Social Work in European Comparison

Forschung, Studium und Praxis

Schriften des Fachbereichs Sozialwesen der
Fachhochschule Münster

Band 13

Waxmann 2008
Münster / New York / München / Berlin

Irmgard Jansen (Ed.)

Social Work
in European Comparison

Waxmann 2008
Münster / New York / München / Berlin

Bibliographic information published by die Deutsche Nationalbibliothek
Die Deutsche Nationalbibliothek lists this publication in the
Deutsche Nationalbibliografie; detailed bibliographic data
are available in the internet at http://dnb.d-nb.de.

Forschung, Studium und Praxis
Schriften des Fachbereichs Sozialwesen
der Fachhochschule Münster, Band 13

ISSN 1435-9839
ISBN 978-3-8309-2016-8

© Waxmann Verlag GmbH, 2008
Postfach 8603, 48046 Münster, Germany

Waxmann Publishing Co.
P. O. Box 1318, New York, NY 10028, U. S. A.

www.waxmann.com
info@waxmann.com

Cover design: Matthias Grunert, Münster
Cover picture: Kevin Kurth, Niederpöcking; www.photocase.com
Typesetting: Stoddart Satz- und Layoutservice, Münster
Print: CCC GmbH, Münster
Printed on age-resistant paper, acid-free as per ISO 9706

Inhalt

Introduction

Even though European universities have implemented BA/MA-degrees, they are far from comparability of their study systems. Moreover, shortening of practice in BA-systems and an increasing economic pressure make it more difficult for students to get practice experiences abroad. However, to compare international experiences seems indispensable if students want to apply for a job throughout Europe.

Demands on a social workers profession emerge against the background of different social, political and cultural developments in different countries. Different systems give shape to profiles of qualifications in social work, thereby closely linked to social-political conditions and their impact on individuals. Against these different backgrounds, models, concepts and methods for teaching and learning professional practice in particular fields of activitiy arise.

At the same time, all European countries have to face up to the challenges of globalized economic orientation, closely connected to questions of education, integration and social participation.

The contributions to this volume are products of a dialogue between six European universities, presented and discussed during an international symposium, organized by the department of Social Work of the University of Applied Sciences, Münster.

Social work scientists coming from Austria, Germany, Norway, Northern Ireland, Poland, and Switzerland presented current developments, concepts and approaches, within the framework of education, poverty, participation, health and social services and against the background of national developments:

– **Margherita Zander**, University of Applied Sciences Münster, explicates action leading consequences, arising from the problems of child poverty. She emphazises the role of social work in the context of compensation, coping and protection and refers to recent resilience research, recommending promotion of resilience, seen "as a process – a dynamic and developmental process in which the children theirselve, their family surrounds and their further social milieu are involved".
– In the first part of his article **Peter Pantucek**, University of Applied Sciences, St. Pölten, clarifies how professional identity of social work in Austria develops against a background of competing and dominating psychotherapy and he points out the tedious process it takes to gain academic recognition. In the second part, the author refers to the development of qualified instruments

of social diagnosis, associated with constructions of professional identity in social work practice. He illustrates graphically how to handle tools like network-cards "used to map personal correlations" and inclusion cards "used as a clearly laid out assessment of the client's degree of inclusion in important societal functional systems".

– **John Duffy**, Queens University Belfast, likewise brings forward user participation in social work education in the Northern Ireland context. He discusses findings of recent research studies examining good practice initiatives as to the involvement of service users and carers.

– **Christan Vogel**, University of Applied Sciences, Bern, Switzerland, presents "forms in which school social work is being institutionalized", seen in a sociological perspective. Analyzing selected case studies, Vogel takes into consideration structure and logics of communication of different actors in this field.

– **Harald Koht**, Oslo University College presents results of a research study on attitudes concerning user participation in municipal child welfare. Recent graduates of programmes in social work of two university colleges were questioned.

– **Iwona Kijowska**, Elblag University of Humanities and Economy, describes types, rights and recruiting processes of foster families in Poland.

– **Irina Sorokosz**, Elblag University of Humanities and Economics, indicates school social work in Poland as a challenging and hard to handle field of professional activity. She expounds the problems of social workers, being at the same time manager, fireman, officer on duty, cop, person for all cases and bosom friend, to devise professionally approved role-patterns.

– **Peter Hansbauer**, University of Applied Sciences, Münster explicates why participation of children and parents in youth work should not be only stated by law, but should be part of the organizational culture in the care planning process.

– **Bernhard Brugger** and **Leander Pflüger**, University of Applied Sciences, Münster call attention to increasing needs to qualify specialists in the fields of health, disease and impairment. They point out that in Germany even today 30% of all qualified social workers are working in the field of health and are challenged to cooperate closely with professional groups, differing in their particular models of health and disease. Advocating a biopsychosocial model, which demands trans- and interdisciplinary approaches to social case work, they aim for qualifying social workers for interdisciplinary thinking and put the question "what understanding of the biopsychosocial model do social workers need to acquire during their training in order to be able to work together with (and successfully assert themselves against) other occupational groups?".

Münster, May 2008   Irmgard Jansen

Childhood Poverty
Consequences for Social Work

Margherita Zander

1. Social Work in the Context of Poverty – Yesterday and Today

"Seldom has a reform of the job market affected the day care facility for children/nursery so directly and on so many levels. Teachers and child carers must be made aware of what the children will be confronted with because Hartz IV also has consequences for the conceptual work in the KiTa (day care facility)."[1]

What was formulated here for the KiTas equally applies to many other areas of pedagogical and social work ... *Historically* speaking the development of social work as a profession is very closely connected with the problem of poverty, in particular, it was always concerned with the effects of poverty on children and youth. That is why it can look back on a long tradition in this connection and would thus be well equipped for this task if it only bears this element of the way it sees itself in mind.

Today, too, social work is variously concerned with poverty in *child* and *youth* and *family help*, *advisory services* on *growing debts* and *debt prevention*, *social work at schools and in certain town quarters,* to mention but a few. It is to be seen in the different socialisation and life worlds of the children – such as family, school, crèche, day care centre (KiTa), town quarter and is, because of its aims, tasks and working methods, challenged more than any other profession to develop conceptual answers to the prevention of the consequences of poverty for children and to practically apply these answers.

---

1 Themenheft zu „Arme Kindheit", Theorie und Praxis der Sozialpädagogik, Heft 3/2005.

1.1 What is New in the Current Challenge by the Growing Problem of Poverty

Up to now social work was *mainly* concerned with the consequences of so-called "old poverty", i.e. with long-term poverty in socially disadvantaged city quarters, with forms of poverty which partly pass from one generation to the next and which frequently *scarcely show any prospects for social rising* – at least for the adult members of the family. It is characteristic for this form of poverty that there is a frequent change between insecure work and receiving social welfare, the poor school and professional qualifications of the parents, few cultural resources and thus barely any possibilities of promoting the children's skills and inclinations. The visible forms of poverty connected with these are more than familiar to the social workers and educational experts, nor can they be overlooked on a daily basis because they are forms of poverty which often leave traces in the persons' outward appearance and in their ways of behaving and in their undeniably multi-problematic situations.

On the other hand, we have had an increasing "new poverty problem" in the Federal Republic of Germany since the 1980s, which displays different traits and which is also partially traceable to other social causes:
– sudden and unexpected unemployment
– separations and divorces (keyword: lone parents)
– as a consequence of cheap jobs
– or because the money from a job does not suffice to provide for a family with several children
– as a result of migrant status, which only permits the lowest social incomes.

Striking features of these "new forms of poverty" are:
– that they are "processes of becoming poor" which represent a more or less sudden invasion into/break in family life,
– that, in contrast to the so-called "old poverty" there are still, in fact, non-material resources, e.g. educational and social resources which can be utilised, but which become used up with time,
– that there is at first the prospect of getting out of this situation, but that social decline cannot be excluded in the long run,
– that people are keen on concealing the visible consequences of poverty to the outward world,
– and that we are dealing with new, less visible forms of poverty that are socio-structurally widely spread and locally not so easy to place.

Experts in education and social work and the institutions of the educational system are, a.o., either not at all or not properly prepared for these forms of poverty which now, and even more so in the future will dominate in numbers.

Moreover, there is also something else: These new forms of poverty, in which many families live together with their children and young people are, both in their quantitative dimension and in the qualitative forms of the way they appear are the expression of a social polarisation process *which is leading to new forms of social exclusion and marginalization.* In fact, it is no longer the material effects of poverty, rather the long-term psycho-social disadvantages which matter individually and socially in a particular way. We must also note that these are processes of becoming poor which reach into the middle classes. The processes of social decline associated with those lead not only to material restrictions in the families concerned, they also trigger off psychodynamic processes by which the various members of the family can be affected in very different ways.

There is in poverty research a tradition of studies which deal with,
– which shifts such processes of social decline and the loss of social status trigger off in internal family relations (e.g.: the shift in the status of fathers when they become unemployed),
– which effects the social restrictions that have become necessary can have on internal family communication and parental styles of bringing up their children, (e.g. increase in restrictive methods of rearing children).

Such processes of "economic deprivation" were, for example, investigated in relation to the World Economic Crisis in the USA by Glen Elder in detail and, following on that, Sabine Walper researched similar processes in the Federal Republic in the 1980s (Elder 1974; Walper 1988). These follow-up psycho-social effects must also be observed from the adult perspective. In the following pages, however, the children should take centre-stage because "Growing up in Poverty" should have light thrown on it as an extreme development risk for children.

1.2 Which Consequences are Emerging for Social Work?

We can indeed say that social work has gone through something of a professional boom in the last thirty years. In the course of this time its *target groups* have grown, its working forms and possibilities have been greatly differentiated. It has moved into the middle of society more strongly overall, also from the introspective point of view and the way it sees itself. The area of children and youth is a very good example of this in which *a* more strongly *preventive task* was transferred to social work by means of the reformulation of the German Law for

Child and Youth Support at the beginning of the 1990s.[2] Thus child and youth aid is now challenged to make a general contribution towards improving the living circumstances of children and young people. Because of this, social work will, in view of the growing problem of poverty, have to reposition itself and, from the way it sees itself, to correspondingly develop a *focus (on the prevention of poverty)*.

To my mind, this implies a challenge on many levels:
- *on a political level* – and this above all affects the sponsors and representatives of the profession – social work is called upon to be fair to its function as lawyer and lobbyist by getting politically involved and by pointing to the effects of the problematic development of a social state again and again (making it seem scandalous as well),
- *on an expert level* – it is a question of developing strategies and concepts for an effective prevention of poverty, respectively, of applying them in a broader framework, which offer both an answer to the individual and family effects, while at the same time working towards structural change. Social work, however, has to face a *basic dilemma* which makes itself more noticeable in times of increased social polarisation: Social work is itself a part of that Social State which is considerably contributing to the increase in the problem of poverty by means of its current political decisions. The Social State which is currently downsizing is, at the same time, its own client, and, as such, it has always given the state the task of working on socially caused problems. Nevertheless, social work was, according to the way it sees itself, at no time merely a taker-on of tasks, it was also a political actor and, as such, keen on putting its own method of problem-solving into effect by means of the ethics and expertise of the profession.

Having said this in advance, I would like in the following to focus in my considerations, *on the one hand* on "Child Poverty as a Problem understood Socio-Pedagogically" and to support my arguments by the current state of knowledge on the perception of, and coping with family poverty from the child's perspective.

On the other hand, I would like to go over to the methods of social work which are related to the support of strategies of coping and the promotion of resilience.

---

2   KJHG: Kinder- und Jugendhilfe-Gesetz, meanwhile SGB VIII = the 8th Chapter of the Code of Social Law.

2. How do Children Experience and Cope With Poverty?

Meanwhile in the Federal Republic of Germany there have been many empirical studies which examined how children deal with their state of family poverty and its very varied effects on themselves. I would like merely to report briefly on the most important insights in this context.

2.1 Survey of the Current State of Knowledge

We know:
- that growing up in poverty can negatively affect both *the present feeling of well-being* and the *child's development prospects,* i.e. his cognitive, emotional and social development.
- that it is, above all, the *social and educational restrictions* as well as the emotional burden by additional family problems (such as separation/ divorce, illness, debts etc.) which make coping with the experience of poverty more difficult.
- that this has to be looked at in a differentiated way according to the *age and development level* of the child and that we have to consider *the temporal and qualitative distinctness* of family poverty (e.g. the accumulation of problem situations).
- that *boys and girls* develop different forms of coping because their gender-specific socialisation influences their coping behaviour.

Thus we know, e.g. from a psychological study by A. Richter (2000) which distinguishes between "problem-avoiding behaviour" and "active problem-solving coping behaviour":
- that, on the one hand, *both boys and girls* living in materially deprived circumstances tend to *"work their problems out for themselves"* or to compensate for restrictions and deficits they experience by means of *"instead-of actions"*;
- that, on the other hand, *girls* are rather more in a position *"to look for social support"* and to create coping resources from their social contacts to their peers or to adults, whereas *boys* are more seldom in a position to do this and tend rather to *"hand over"* their problems *"to their surrounds."*

Problem-avoiding coping models:
- "working it out for themselves" (e.g.: reducing their claims, withdrawal ...)
- carrying out "instead-of actions" (e.g.: devaluing others, consuming impulsively).

Problem-solving coping models:

–   "looking for or granting emotional support" (e.g. supporting one another, looking for help/allies)

–   "putting it off on their surrounds" (e.g.: reacting impulsively, making demands, stealing, acting fraudulently).

Studies on child poverty at primary school age in which I participated (Chassé, Zander & Rasch 2007), but also other studies, such as that of the ISS[3], showed, above all:

–   that children *with similar material starting points* develop different coping strategies and ways of dealing with their problems, i.e. that we are concerned with a wide spectrum of child coping strategies;

–   that the children's different forms of coping can be explained by means of a complex *interaction of structurally given framework conditions and subjective coping possibilities;*

–   that, as far as the children are concerned, *the parents' behaviour* (both in the way they cope with everyday problems as well as in the way they perceive their prospects), the parents' patterns of coping with their situation have a decisive (mediatory) function.

2.2 Child Coping Strategies: Attempt of a Typology

We did, indeed, in our study, find a broad spectrum of coping strategies among the pre-school children we questioned which ranged from "*barely restricted by the desperate situation*" to "*multiply disadvantaged, respectively, neglected*" *children.* With regard to the typification, we paid particular attention to how the children manage to deal with *tasks connected with their development in their various life worlds, i.e. in their family, at school and in their peer group* in a manner appropriate to their age. The typification thus carried out was intended to show which outward circumstances burden the children, or which ones support them in coping with their poverty.

Type 1: Family poverty – child compensation

We came upon, in this context, on the one hand, a group of "fit" children, who, seemingly undisturbed by their materially difficult life situation appear to cope well with their development tasks in all three areas of socialisation (family, school and relations to their peer group). We noted a series of stimulating aspects, so-called protective factors.

---

3   ISS=Institut of Social Education and Social Work in Frankfurt.

Type 2: Multiple burdening of the family – Children in strongly and multiply disadvantaged life situations

On the other hand, one group of children stood out who may be evaluated as "multiply disadvantaged and partly neglected." The children of this type must come to terms with considerable deficits in their everyday structures and show great difficulties in coping with their development tasks. It is striking that these children to a great extent lack boosting or protective factors.

Type 3: Multiply differentiated mid-fielders with different disadvantages

Apart from those already mentioned, there is a *third group of children* who have a combination of burdening and relieving structures in their everyday child life and in their family life. Categorising this group of children in the *middle field* is rather difficult because these children tend, in their coping behaviour, to belong partly to Type 1 and partly to Type 2. Nevertheless, a closer consideration of this group can lead to interesting insights in the question of possibilities of prevention and intervention:

1. Children profit from their mother's (or parents') actively organising their social network and from the formers' enabling them to develop.
2. Children partly find *compensating possibilities themselves,* e.g. in the framework of school, in the extended circle of family with the grandparents, with fathers living separately etc.
3. Children profit from *their own social nets,* they can be supported in their coping strategies by positive contacts to their peers.
4. Children have recourse to the *compensating possibilities of institutions*, e.g. school and day-care centres (KiTas) can make social contacts and cultural experiences possible and many disadvantages can be counterbalanced by institutions related to child and youth help (Chassé, Zander & Rasch 2007).

Thus the important role of institutions and social work in the context of coping with poverty is made clear. In summary, we can assume the following from the state of knowledge and experience hitherto:

There *are burdening and relieving factors* – or, as research in resilience describes it, risk and protective factors – which offer an explanation for why children starting from materially comparable situations such as poverty cope with these in completely different ways.

It is important for us to focus more acutely on the burdening or relieving factors in the individual children's areas of socialisation to be able to derive *conclusions for professional pedagogical and social scientific work* from them:

Relieving and supporting factors:
–   Constructive parental coping strategies
–   Supportive and sympathetic parent-child relationship
–   Supportive social networks in the circle of relatives and friends (of the parents)
–   Positive social contacts of the children (above all, relationships with peers)
–   Stimulating offers of institutions (e.g. school, care centre, children's meeting places) close to home

Burdening and restricting factors:
–   Ambivalent or negative coping strategies
–   Lacking parental sympathy and ability to support
–   Parental inability to cope, particularly because of additional burdening problems (such as separation, divorce, addiction, sickness, debts, family violence, social isolation of the family)
–   Negative social contacts (exclusion and stigmatisation)
–   Over-demanding structures in institutions, incapable of recognising the problem of poverty (e.g. over-demanding teaching in school etc.)

When contrasting risk and protective factors, *needs for action on various levels and in the most varied socialisation and life worlds of the children* become clear. This represents a challenge for all social professions which are in contact or work with these children and their families, especially with regard to social work, which I shall restrict myself to in the following.

3.   Child Poverty – a Challenge for Social Work

Just as the effects of poverty on children and their families manifest themselves in a complex manner, the consequences for social-political and social pedagogical measures we derive from them would have to be discussed. Social work is – as mentioned at the beginning – confronted with child and family poverty in various contexts and can certainly fall back on a wide area of methodical and conceptual knowledge based on experience.

I would like – in view of the increasing problem of poverty – *to prioritise poverty prevention and, in concrete terms, the new discussion on the demand for resilience.*

3.1 Poverty Prevention as an Overall Concept

In general, poverty prevention aims at *avoiding negative consequences of poverty* and builds on the promotion of resources and potentials which are already in existence or have still to be acquired. The general social-political and social-pedagogical aim of the action would have to be: *"Strengthening the strengths and limiting the weaknesses."*

Basically we distinguish between *three levels of prevention* which can also be transferred to poverty prevention (Zander 2004):
- *Primary Prevention* aims to avoid a risk arising, which would mean, in our case, *avoiding child poverty*, i.e. creating extended possibilities of access to poverty-preventing resources (income, waged work, education, health, housing, social and cultural share). No doubt, social work has possibilities in relation to this of supporting access to such resources in the individual case. However, I see in this an original political task which touches all levels, from the communal, via the state (Land) and the federal level to the European level.
- *Secondary Prevention* works from a starting point in which *the risk – in our case the risk of poverty – has arisen*, thus leading to acute endangerment. Prevention means in this context *staving off the acute or potential consequences of the endangerment,* i.e. avoiding negative effects on child life at present and the future development of the children concerned, or at least minimising them. To my mind, above all for this area, conclusions may be drawn from the insights into the various coping constellations.
- It is the aim of *Tertiary Prevention* to take *precautionary measures against the risk arising repeatedly.* In relation to poverty as a life situation, this could be interpreted as averting the danger of *long-term poverty* or even *passing it socially down the generations.*
- The decisive question for Tertiary Prevention can thus be expressed: How can the so-called "vicious circle of poverty" be broken? What possibilities are there to take an influence on the children who grow up in such long-term poverty to help them find a way out of the poverty?
- Admittedly, we are dealing here with a rather more traditional area of social-scientific and social-pedagogical possibilities. In so far, it is not, first and foremost, a question of developing new concepts, rather of evaluating or increasing *the preventive effect of existing concepts* (I think of projects in

different town quarters) *to tie them into an overall graded concept of poverty prevention.* It is important that such concepts be applied *simultaneously at all three levels:*

– for the child, to give them access to coping potentials
– for the family and especially the parents, to strengthen their ability to cope and to bring up their children
– in the child's extended social milieu, which includes e.g. school, day centre, neighbourhood and the town quarter, in order to mobilise resources which support successful coping.

These are just those levels at which concepts for promoting resilience begin with the aim to strengthen the children's and families' ability to resist and thus to have an influence on the structures of the community, so that it also spreads resilience-boosting effects.

3.2 Boosting Resilience as a Method of Poverty Prevention

"The characteristics of the children capable of resilience which are favourable to life and the support which they were given in their family and community were the steps of a spiral staircase which, with every step, led the child to being able to cope successfully with their life. Their path of life was not always straight, rather upwardly directed, the final point was a confident human being capable of achievement who looks hopefully into the future." (Werner 1999, p. 31)

The insight achieved into *child poverty* regarding the relieving and burdening factors is confirmed, if in a more complexly elaborated form, in the rather more psychologically less social-pedagogically oriented *resilience research*. This branch of research can in the meantime – above all in the Anglo-American area – look back on a history of more than thirty years and has, on various occasions, made a topic of *"poverty as a central risk in the development"* of children. That is why it seems reasonable to increasingly refer to it recently when looking for effective concepts of poverty prevention.

We mean by *"resilience" the psychic ability to resist* which expresses itself when children, in spite of unfavourable circumstances and a wide variety of disadvantages (development risks), develop, contrary to expectations, "healthily", i.e., from a psychological point of view, they are not conspicuous in their behaviour, nor have they anything psychopathological about them and are able to cope with the development tasks commensurate to their age. By means of their successful coping with challenges, they also develop other abilities which can prove to be personal resources or lend them competence in dealing with "new risks" (c.f. spiral staircase).

Resilience is thus *not a congenital characteristic,* it is rather an ability which can be acquired when tackling burdens and unfavourable circumstances and which *can,* above all, *be promoted.* Resilience cannot, however, be put on a par with invulnerability. Children can prove themselves resilient towards the effects of certain risks, but not towards others. This ability to resist must also be acquired again and again although the likelihood of resilient behaviour increases with every positive experience (picture of the upward spiral staircase). Children who have gone through such processes are thus *not invulnerable,* they simply do not give in so easily. From a *social-pedagogical perspective,* it is thus more appropriate to see resilience as a *process* – a dynamic adaptive and developmental process in which *the children theirself, their family surrounds and their further social milieu* are involved.

The point of reference for research into resilience – and the concepts for promoting resilience derived from that – thus form risk- and protection factors which can both be individually located on the above-mentioned levels. In this resilience is created as a result of a complex interplay of risk- and protective factors, i.e. risk- and protective factors do not necessarily annul one another, they rather create complex interactions between the two.

In relation to the effects of protective factors, different models are being discussed which offer useful tips for the development of social-pedagogical concepts of action (Wustmann 2004):

1. The *compensation model* means that risk factors can be reduced (or neutralised) in their effect, i.e. that they have a direct influence on the child's process of development.
2. The *challenging model* works on the basis that positive coping with risks (or stress factors) increases the ability to be resilient (picture of an upwardly winding spiral staircase).
3. The *protective factor model* attributes a moderating function to protective factors, implying interaction between risk and protective factors, i.e. protective factors develop a stronger effect if there is a risk involved.

These models do not exclude one another, indeed they can rather be seen as mutually complementary. The assumptions which are their basis were proven in several empirical studies. The most widely spread at present is, however, the protective factor model.

Following these models, different intervention strategies can be applied in promoting resilience: At first it continues to be a matter of *reducing risks,* i.e. bearing the children's vulnerability in mind and reducing their recognisable risks and stress factors. The main focus is, however, laid on *resource-oriented strategies* and on *mobilising protective processes* to thus strengthen the child's ability to be resilient.

According to the insights that risk- and protective factors must be seen on different levels, *promotion of resilience starts on these three levels* (Grotberg 2003):

a) directly with the child

i.e. by promoting basic skills/factors of resilience, for which there are specifically elaborated concepts;

b) on the relationship level

i.e., above all, strengthening parental skills with regard to bringing their children up and their ability to relate to their children, and there are many different concepts for parental training (e.g.: German Association for the Protection of Children);

c) on the structural level/ in the town quarter

i.e. promoting supporting factors in the child's extended social milieu, which involves using and developing the concepts of the community work.

These are precisely the three levels on which social work in promoting the resilience of children in situations of poverty could start. There are also, meanwhile, a lot of different projects in the Federal Republic of Germany – as e.g. the "Moki" in Mohnheim or also the two Model Projects in Saarbrücken (Malstatt und Altsaarbrücken).

Let me in conclusion just highlight the scheme for promoting resilience developed by Edith Grotberg. How should we imagine a resilient child? Where can we start promoting resilience?

A resilient child says: (Groteberg's Scheme, Grotberg 2003)

I have (outer support)
- people who trust and love me,
- people who set me limits (orientation and protection from dangers),
- people who are my models and from whom I can learn,
- people who support and confirm me in acting independently,
- people who help me when I am sick or in danger and who support me in learning new things.

I am (inner strength)
- a child who is appreciated and loved,
- happy to be able to help others and to signal my sympathy for them,
- respectful towards myself and others,

- conscious of my responsibility for what I do,
- confident that everything will turn out alright.

I can (interpersonal skills and ability to solve problems)
- speak to others when something frightens or worries me,
- find solutions for problems with which I am confronted,
- control my behaviour in difficult situations,
- feel when it is right to act independently or to seek the opportunity to speak to someone,
- find someone who helps me when I need support.

One final remark:
Promoting resilience does not eliminate the socially deplorable state of affairs of child and family poverty. It can, however, make a contribution to limiting the negative effects in the families and children affected by it (Zander 2008).

References

Chassé, K. A., Zander, M. & Rasch, K. (2007): Meine Familie ist arm. Wie Kinder im Grundschulalter Armut erleben und bewältigen, 3rd ed., Wiesbaden.

Elder, G. H. (1974): Children of the Great Depression: Social Change in Life Experience, Chicago: University Press.

Grotberg, E. H. (2003): What Is Resilience? How Do You Promote It? How Do You Use It?, In: E. H. Grotberg (ed.): Resilience for Today. Gaining Strength from Adversity, 2nd ed., Westport.

Richter, A. (2000): Wie erleben und bewältigen Kinder Armut? Eine qualitative Studie über die Belastungen aus Unterversorgungslagen und ihre Bewältigung aus subjektiver Sicht von Grundschulkindern einer ländlichen Region, Aachen.

Walper, S. (1988): Familiäre Konsequenzen ökonomischer Deprivation, München/ Weinheim.

Werner, E. (1999): Entwicklung zwischen Risiko und Resilienz, In: G. Opp, M. Fingerle & A. Freytag (eds.), Was Kinder stärkt. Erziehung zwischen Risiko und Resilienz, München/Basel.

Wustmann, C. (2004): Resilienz. Widerstandsfähigkeit von Kindern in Tagesein-richtungen fördern, Weinheim/Basel.

Zander, M. (2004): Spielräume und Bewältigungshandeln von (armen) Kindern – Erste Schlussfolgerungen für Armutspräventionsarbeit, Referat auf der Arbeitstagung „Eine Allianz für Kinder – Ansätze und Wirkung von Armutsprävention", ISS, Frankfurt, November 2004.

Zander, M. (2008): Armes Kind – starkes Kind. Die Chance der Resilienz, Wiesbaden.

The University of Applied Sciences St. Pölten and the Identity of Social Work in Austria[1]

Peter Pantucek

Dear ladies and gentlemen!

Right at the start I have to tell you that I will not quite stick to the announcement in the agenda and will report only a bit about diagnostics, but a lot about the activities and the University of Applied Sciences in St. Pölten. I hope that you will excuse my straying off the topic.

I come from St. Pölten, from a small university. Our department has set itself the ambitious goal of implementing social work science in Austria, in a strong correlation with the practice of social work. We do not only strive to establish ourselves in the scientific communities with our efforts and to find our niche in there. We also want to influence the development of a professional culture of social work in Austria.

1. Social Work Science Research and Development at the University of Applied Sciences St. Pölten

It is only since 2001 that social work has been taught at university level in Austria. Before that, the educational programmes were integrated in the vocational school system and the "Academy for Social Work" was a postsecondary educational institution. It was not entitled to confer academic titles and had neither a research assignment, nor the financial means to participate in research or theory development.

Nevertheless the team in St. Pölten did research, even under those unfavourable conditions, and participated actively in discussions about the alignment of social work. We understand social work as a profession aligned to the client's every day

---

1   Presentation on the Symposium in Münster.

living situation, interested in the living conditions of the disadvantaged and working on improving them. We consider social work as community orientated and would like to distinguish ourselves from "psychologizing" tendencies. Our special focus lies on issues of methodology.

The establishment of social work studies at the University of Applied Sciences in 2002 equals an integration into the system of academic education. This development is further promoted by the Bologna process – in future every student of social work will have access to the whole range of academic qualifications. Currently we are also working on the establishment of social work PhD programs, for the time being in international cooperations.

The establishment of social work studies in the academic system has led to a significant improvement of social work research. Research departments have been developed parallel to the Austrian study courses, first results are already available.

The team at the University of Applied Sciences St. Pölten has extended it research activities systematically in the last years. In 2007 we founded the Ilse Arlt Institute on Social Inclusion Research, which coordinates the social work science research and the theory development at the University of Applied Sciences and is responsible for the linking up of the research results and the teaching.

According to our understanding, the recorded professional expertise, often represented in organisation-internal papers and concepts, is already a rudimentary form of the reflexion and systematisation of the professional practice. Social work science is interested in this reflexion and contributes to it by providing tools for practice. It is our task to provide tools for reflexion and tools for devising strategies and to contribute to the extension of the front line social workers' capacity to act. I will get back to the question how we are doing this a bit later.

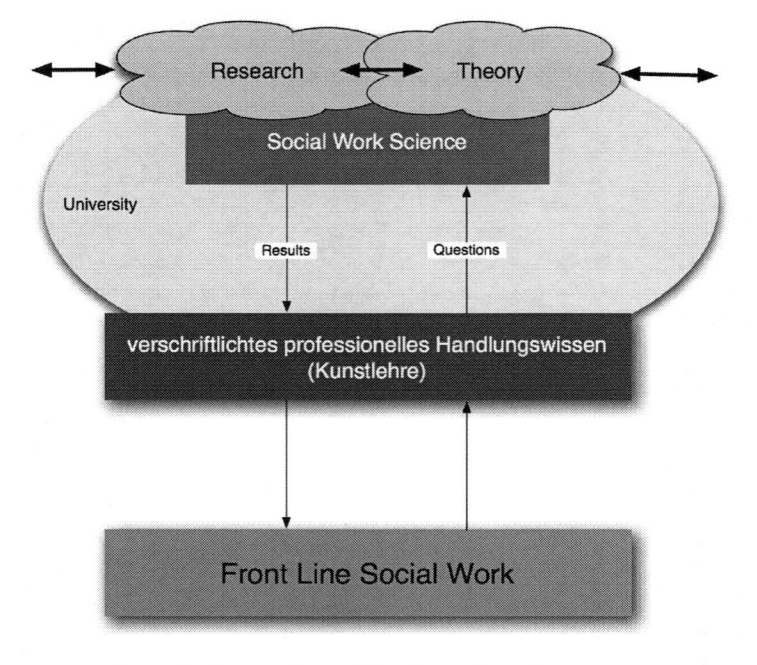

Below you see the main focus points of the Ilse Arlt Institute:

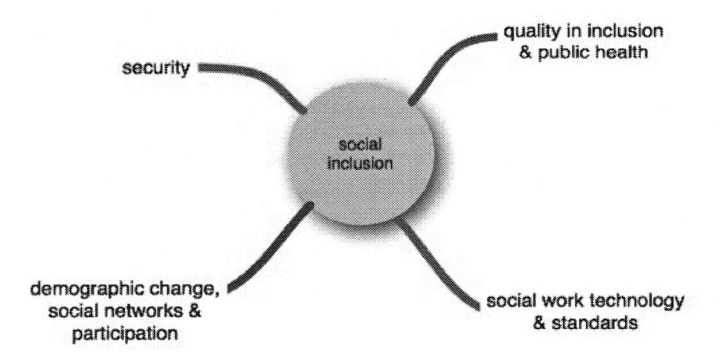

Figure 1: Focus points of the Ilse Arlt Institute

Each of these focus points is considered in context with issues of social inclusion. When dealing with issues of security, we are interested in combining approaches to increase the security in communities and the public space with measures to promote inclusion. In cooperation with the Austrian Railways we are trying to get financial aid for a scheme to increase safety at railway stations, which also aims to prevent the social marginalisation of disadvantaged groups like the homeless in the public space and/or to develop alternatives. In rural areas, residents are concerned about the occurrence of phenomena which so far have been considered typically urban, as for example the consumption of illegal drugs, vandalism, isolation and social segregration.

Our understanding of social work sees it embedded in a social environment and as a contribution to the shaping of democracy. This is also the reason why we are interested in the development of natural social networks under the conditions of the demographic change of the modern society.

In cooperation with two other universities and independent providers we are developing an extensive agenda which will be completed shortly, comprising guidelines for a quality oriented tendering of social services.

In the course of a subproject we are analyzing cases of foster care for children and adolescents. We interview the children/adolescents, their parents, the social workers, their carers and research their files. The results of this analysis by a multi-professional team leads to the development of quality criteria.

We are also really proud of a project which we call "social environment oriented short-term intervention". In short counselling and facilitating processes we support rural communities and protagonists of social work in finding their own ways to promote inclusion of citizens. In these communities we apply a method which resembles closely short case interventions.

According to our understanding, the term "social work technology" refers to techniques of counselling, of diagnosing and of organising support processes. We are developing diagnostic methods and in cooperation with software experts at our university we are trying to develop software solutions involving clients in the diagnostic process. In this process we understand the social diagnosis as a unity of diagnosis and counselling.

In the years to come, teaching and training material for social work interviewing and counselling is to be developed. In order to achieve this goal, we have prioritised counselling and interviewing training in the Bachelor programme on the one hand, on the other hand required technical equipment will be available to us in a state-of the-art language laboratory as of the following winter semester.

These are the most important lines of our method development work. We have a keen interest in transacting at least part of our research programmes in international cooperations.

2.   Social Work Identity Problems in Austria

Now I would like to deal with problems of social work identity in Austria. After all I am supposed to address also the issue which is the title of my presentation.

The last 20 years have been quite turbulent for the social work profession. The 80s were characterised by "therapizing" tendencies. Further education provision in social work was dominated, some time even monopolised by psychotherapy. Since social workers did not have access to studies leading to academic degrees, the training to become a psychotherapist used to be one of the few options to achieve a higher professional qualification. At the same time the trainings offered corresponded to a trend both in social work and the general public opinion. Social workers disrespected their own qualification, for many it was nothing but a stopover to the "actual" professional help, which was considered to be therapy. A gradual erosion of the profession's self-confidence and an increasing lack of clarity about the social work specific contribution to the societal support system and for the clients could be observed.

In the 90ies this trend slowly came to end. Towards the end of the 90s, for the first time social workers were provided access to academic degrees by social management training courses. Managerial perspectives established themselves as relevant interpretative models of the profession. Yet the main task of social work, the working with clients, could hardly profit from this approach. It is true that more and more social workers were able to establish themselves on the executive level of provider organisations. But in many cases their understanding for the intrinsic logic of support process had become insufficient. They seemed to have changed their identity – or seemed to have found a professional identity for the first time, but one that did not have much to do with social work anymore.

Within the scope of establishment of study courses at the Universities of Applied Sciences, the social work practitioners have become more and more insecure. They are afraid that their qualifications might be devaluated and have strong reservations against a more scientific alignment of the study courses. They are concerned that the graduates of the Universities of Applied Sciences will not be willing to do practical social work and that they will not be genuinely interested in their clients. In their opinion, social work identity, which has always been precarious anyway, is at risk.

As a matter of fact, the students are provided with a more profound education nowadays. Today they have learned more, when they enter the practical social work. But there they prove their ability at least to the same extent as their predecessors.

Now we provide shortened master studies for practitioners. Their previous education is accredited as an equivalent of a Bachelor degree. Some of the most dedicated practitioners attend these study courses, but the vast majority of social workers remain uninterested. The profession starts to become more differentiated also in Austria.

Our recent focus on tools of social diagnostic, a practice which has been neglected for many years, has far-reaching consequences. By teaching established and newly developed diagnostic methods which help to address precisely the correlation between the individual and the societal resources, we provide our colleagues with a tool which strengthens their professional identity. They are now able to position themselves in contrast to the neighbouring professions in multi-professional teams and are able to present their assessments in a more substantiated way.

Two tools have proved especially successful: The first one is not new at all, but used to be widely unknown in Austrian social work. It is the network card, used to map personal correlations. The second tool has been developed by me. It is called "inclusion card" and facilitates a clearly laid out assessment of the client's degree of inclusion in important societal functional systems.

Whereas the network card is a tool belonging to the cooperative diagnostic system, i.e. developed in cooperation with the client and allows for network card counselling, the inclusion card is a tool which enables social workers to make a recapitulating assessment of the client's situation and helps them to substantiate their intervention decisions.

At first, let's talk about network cards. We apply a model which consistently uses no more than four sectors, one sector for family relations, one for friends/ neighbours relations, one for colleague relations and one for professional relations. We consistently assess relations only in context with their closeness/distance to the "ego", the anchor person. The reason for this limitation is that the ambivalence of relations, which can be at the same time supporting and/or restricting should not be eliminated by a rash evaluation or categorisation. The development potential and the ambivalence of relations are topics of counselling.

In the following I would like to show you some examples of network cards.

The first example is the network card of a 23-year old woman. She is socially well integrated. The network card features a considerable extent and a moderate density in the three sectors family, friends/neighbours and colleagues.

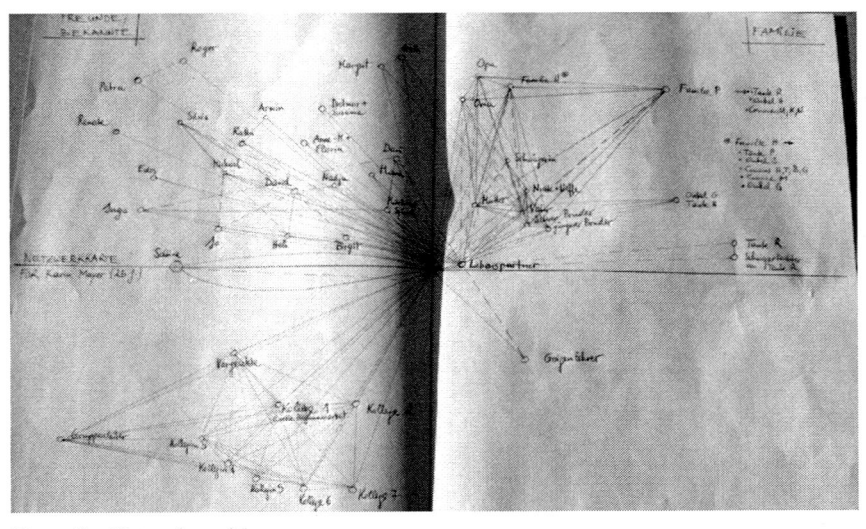

Figure 2: Network card 1

The second example: the network of a 25-year old man. There are not many family relations, and no friends/neighbours relations at all. The colleague relations are strongly connected to the professional relations. The disabled young man works in a sheltered workshop.

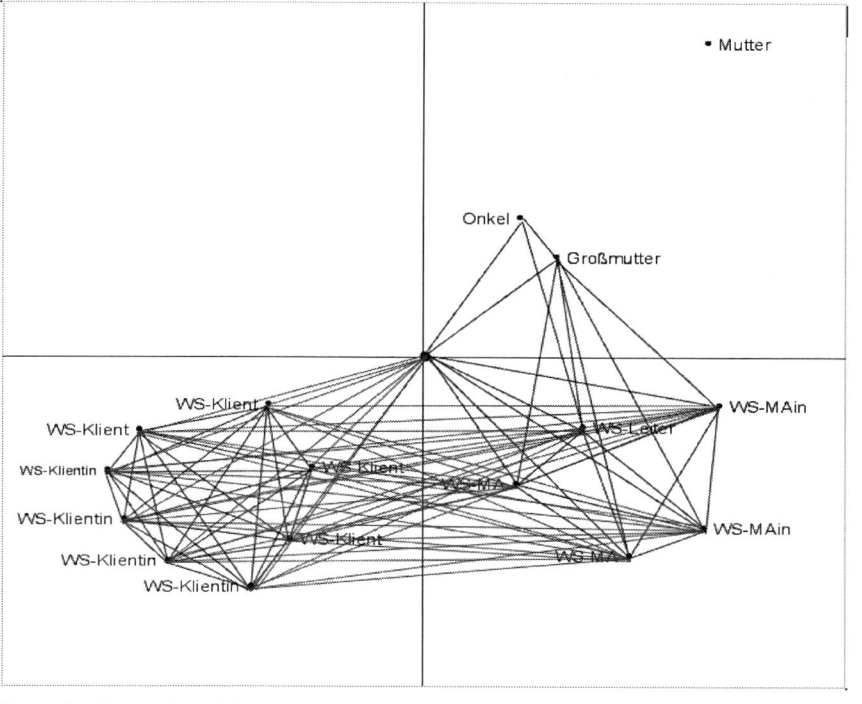

Figure 3:   Network card 2

Here we can see, how professional and professionally controlled relations substitute the natural network of relations. We can also see that the relation to his mother has been broken off. We do not obtain any information about his father. Our thesis is that in cases like this one, the standard procedure of social and health care institutions devaluates and thins out natural networks. We consider the counteracting of the deformation of ego-centered networks by undesired side-effects of societal support as a task of social work.

The third example shows this thinning out of natural networks even more clearly. It is the diagram of the network of a 20-year old woman, who has gone though a schizophrenic episode.

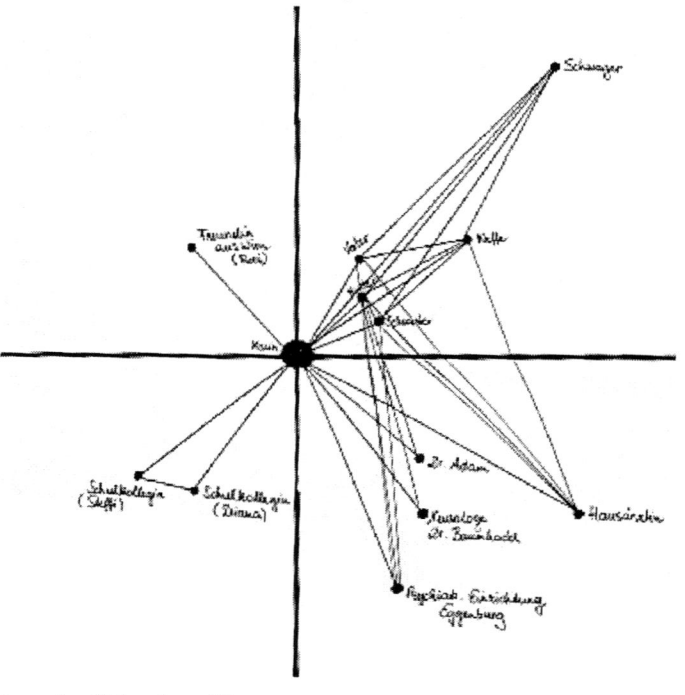

Figure 4:   Network card 3

Here we can see the beginning of the client's complete isolation. The relationships on the left half of the network card are only being maintained via e-mail.

We consider the distinction between family relations a further consequence of professional interventions: close relatives are often contaced by professionals and therefore gain significance and come closer to the anchor persons. Other relatives are usually not contacted and not involved in the considerations, they are marginalized. This effect seems to be especially strong in child protection services. This is the reason why we consider Peter Hansbauer's project to try out the family conference meetings and/or the family group decision making models in Germany especially significant.

We would like to utilise network cards also to a larger extent for network related research. We are working on a user-friendly software solution which will facilitate the generation of network cards by the clients themselves and will automatise the mathematical analysis. Thus we obtain data which we can use for the research and which will contribute to the optimisation of social work intervention strategies.

And now the second tool for a social diagnosis, which also seems to prove its worth in practical social work. The inclusion card outlines complex pieces of information on a client's situation and circumstances, displays them on a distinct chart and serves as a substantiation of intervention and non-intervention decisions.

Inclusion-Chart								
Client						Created by		Created on
Presenting Problem								
Functional System	Degree of Inclusion					Tendency	Characteristics	Measures
	full	to a large extent	partly	excluded	perm. e.			
A. Employment								
B. Social Insurance								
C. Money Matters								
D. Mobility								
E. Education								
F. Access to Information								
G. Health Care								
H. Social Support								

Attempts to popularise Karls' and Wandrei's PIE as a classification system for social work in the German speaking areas have failed so far. There is a distinct lack of a tool to substantiate professional assessments. Referring to the current system theory discourse, I have developed this graph displaying the client's inclusion in functional systems significant for the safeguarding of one's life situation and one's social involvement. Inclusion always has to be considered as a relation between individual and societal conditions. For example, the inclusion in the health system can either fail due to the lack of adequate provisions or due to the client's fear of medical treatments and hospital admissions, as in the following example:

Inclusion-Chart

Client	Franziska Czech, 42a					Created by: DSA Leitner	Created on: x.x.2003
Presenting Problem	(Self Diagnosis) Episode of Depression						

Functional System	Degree of Inclusion					Tendency	Characteristics	Measures
	full	to a large extent	partly	excluded	perm. e.			
A. Employment		X				=	Precarious labour relations, hardly discontinuities	none
B. Social Insurance	X					=	Permanently insured	none
C. Money Matters	X					=	Cash card, no significant debts (according to client)	maybe check later
D. Mobility		X				–	No car, using public transport is becoming more and more difficult	see factor G
E. Education		X				=	no educational activities for the last 15 years, willingness existent	suggest courses?
F. Access to Information		X				+	TV, does not read newspapers, now active search (coming to counselling).	none
G. Health Care		X				– !!!	access possible, refuses medical consultations (adiposity?) worrying symptoms	coaching
H. Social Support			X			–	virtually no existing relationships, embarrassment	network counselling and reconstruction

Chart 1: Inclusions-Chart Examplel 1

This tool avoids any allocations of blame, and therefore does not lead to the client's stigmatisation. Yet it diagnoses social work relevant circumstances of exclusion.

In addition to the degree of inclusion, the tendency is recorded. The current tendency highlights critical developments. In this example, this applies to dimension G, the health care system. As a rule, in the case of acute exclusion tendencies an intervention should be carried out immediately, the next step are interventions at other exclusion tendencies, supplemented by a positive tendency, if existent. More than three dimensions should not be in the focus of interventions simultaneously.

Both, the network card and the inclusion chard are well received and welcomed by colleagues testing them in practical work. These tools do not only support the counselling and the focussing of interventions, but also help practitioners to define their professional identity more clearly. They make clear that social work means working on the client's societal inclusion. They enable you to contribute structured and methodologically supported expertise into the interdisciplinary cooperation with doctors, psychologists and representatives of other neighbouring professions.

Résumé

Now I have presented to you our research and development work at the University of Applied Sciences St. Pölten. I have exemplified our efforts to promote the development of professionality in social work by describing methods developed and publicised by us. We are striving for international cooperation's for our projects which we are planning to pursue for the following years.

I hope I could arouse your interest and thank you very much for your attention.

Citizen Involvement in Social Work Education in the Northern Ireland Context

Joe Duffy

Abstract

This paper and presentation discusses the findings of research undertaken recently in Northern Ireland which examines good practice initiatives in the involvement of service users and carers in social work education. The findings from this study may have relevance to social work education providers in other European contexts where the involvement of social work service users (clients) and caregivers is being considered.

The introduction of the new Honours Degree in Social Work in Northern Ireland in September 2004 heralded an opportunity for service users and carers as citizens to play a significant role in the training of social work students. In its Framework Specification for the Degree in Social Work (2003), the Department of Health, Social Services and Public Safety (DHSSPS) clearly articulates its expectations around the importance of the service user and carers contributing to social work education at strategic and operational levels.

In addition this framework specification also requires social work students to demonstrate an understanding of what is referred to as the *Northern Ireland Context* where social work students are required to understand:

"the personal and community consequences of the Northern Ireland conflict for individuals, families, groups, and communities and the implications for social work practice" (DHSSPS 2003, p. 16).

Citizen Involvement in Social Work Education in the Northern Ireland Context (Duffy 2006) is a good practice guide which has been co-written with service users and carers. Its purpose is to complement established good practice initiatives in the involvement of such citizens in social work training on social work degree programmes in Northern Ireland. Based on research conducted with service users, carers, students, agency and academic partners, the guide focuses on the key values which need to accompany such involvement as well as including case studies of good practice to show how citizens have been effectively involved to date at all levels of social work training in Northern Ireland.

Furthermore, this guide importantly addresses ways in which service users and carers as citizen trainers can contribute to social work students understanding issues around the *Northern Ireland context,* i.e. how people have been affected by a protracted period of conflict in this country.

Introduction

When social work training in Northern Ireland was reformed with the introduction of the social work degree in 2004, it marked the beginning for social work students needing to address issues associated with Northern Ireland's conflict as part of their social work studies. Before this, students were only expected to demonstrate *awareness* of issues associated with anti-racist and anti-oppressive perspectives as a broader dimension of their understanding of social work values. Non-sectarian perspectives were seen as an integral aspect of the latter.

However, it would be fair to say that the background of Northern Ireland's *Troubles,* the term euphemistically used to describe the conflict in the country, have always presented complexities and challenges for both qualified social workers and students alike about openly talking about controversial and challenging subjects such as sectarianism in this way. Some commentators would go as far as suggesting that this type of dialogue would have presented real dangers to practitioners in many circumstances (Smyth & Campbell 1996).

To some extent, this may help explain why Northern Ireland's public sector, the largest employer of social workers, adopted a policy stance of neutrality in terms of its working relationships and practices. It was intended that this would deter employees from having to engage in any discussion associated with the devastation going on around them.

The social work degree in Northern Ireland was then introduced in September 2004 at a time of peace and normality. Its curricular requirement that students needed to demonstrate an understanding of what is referred to as *'the Northern Ireland Context'* reflected a broader societal move in Northern Ireland and in social work as a profession towards more openness about engagement with issues such as sectarianism. This would have previously been more difficult and hard to imagine. This *Northern Ireland Context* knowledge requirement is addressed by the Northern Ireland Social Care Council (NISCC), the regulatory Body for social work in Northern Ireland, in its guidance for the Social Work Degree (DHSSPS 2003) where it states:

"... the impact of past and current violence, conflict and divisions in Northern Irish society requires particular emphasis in the education and training of social work students in Northern Ireland" (DHSSPS 2003, p. 6).

Another novel aspect of social work education in Northern Ireland and in the United Kingdom more broadly was around the involvement of service users (social work clients) and carers (informal and unpaid caregivers) in all aspects and levels of social work degree provision, both strategically and operationally. Although the NISCC provided curriculum guidance on how the *Northern Ireland Context* could be delivered as a discrete knowledge requirement in the social work curriculum, there was no mention as to how such service users and carers might equally contribute in this important area.

The author therefore secured research funding from the Higher Education Academy Subject Centre for Social Work and Social Policy (SWAP), based at the University of Southampton, United Kingdom, to develop and publish good practice guidelines on ways in which service users and carers as citizen trainers could contribute to social work training and also enhance students' understanding of the Northern Ireland Context. The study was also supported by the Social Care Institute for Excellence (SCIE, London) and the NISCC (Belfast).

The findings from the work are expanded upon in this paper and can be used as guidance for our European partners who wish to explore ways for both involving social work clients in social work education generally and also in helping students understand the impact of conflict from the service user's own unique experiential perspective.

Northern Ireland – Background

Considerable research and commentary have been undertaken around the political conflict in Northern Ireland, particularly for the period from the mid 1960s until the present. Northern Ireland's violent conflict lasted over 30 years and left more than 3700 people dead, many thousands injured and many people and communities both deeply traumatized and psychologically injured (Duffy 2006).

Until the signing of the peace accord known as the Good Friday/Belfast Agreement in 1998, Northern Ireland, to many observers, had the reputation as being both a *place apart* in the United Kingdom and one of the most violent societies in Western Europe. With a population of over 1.7 million people, Northern Ireland is constitutionally part of the United Kingdom but separate from the Republic of Ireland. Both citizenship, political identity and national allegiance have all been contested issues in Northern Ireland since it was separated from the Republic of Ireland through partition in 1921 (CCETSW 1998, p. 4). However, these differences are additionally complicated by the fact that many of Northern Ireland's large minority of Catholics see themselves as Irish with aspirations towards the re-unification of Ireland, and a Protestant majority perceiving itself as British, which seeks ongoing maintenance of the constitutional links with Britain.

Whilst these difficulties cannot be underestimated, the 1998 Peace Agreement was symbolic of a new beginning in Northern Ireland with both the United Kingdom and Ireland governments committing themselves to "... the achievement of reconciliation, tolerance, mutual trust, and the protection and vindication of the human rights of all" (Governments of UK and Ireland 1998). For its part, the social work profession has not been unaffected by these circumstances.

Social Work in Northern Ireland

Social work has had to absorb and manage the many uncertainties and challenges accompanying service delivery in a divided society such as large-scale population movements, intimidation of families and the influence of paramilitary organizations (Williamson & Darby 1978).

During the period of Direct Rule government from Westminster, London (1972-1998) different phases in policy makers' responses to ongoing political violence also emerged in Northern Ireland (Pinkerton & Campbell 2002). For example, the introduction of an integrated health and social services system in 1973 occurred at the time when social workers across the UK began to train generically. Pinkerton suggests however that the introduction of this integrated service in Northern Ireland helped cultivate potential obstacles for social workers to directly engage with difficult and controversial subject matter such as sectarianism. Instead, Pinkerton contends that "... this 'technocratisation' of services ... provided an environment in which staff coming from both sides of the community could distance themselves from the sectarianism of the wider society and develop a non-sectarian professional identity" (CCETSW 1998, p. 22).

The climate of peace however from the mid nineties has helped reduce this distance in terms of social workers feeling more at ease about addressing hitherto uncomfortable subjects. One example of how social workers would be assisted with this was through the publication in 1999 of a range of standards in practice and training aimed at offering practical suggestions as to how social workers and their employers might examine aspects of sectarianism in a more open, safe environment in Northern Ireland (CCETSW 1999). By 2004, the Batchelor in Social Work was introduced at a time of continuing peace in Northern Ireland. This qualification had explicit expectations about social work students being better equipped and prepared for engaging with divisive issues such as sectarianism through their training than was the experience of their student predecessors. It is therefore hoped that social work students will be better prepared for undertaking more progressive modes of engagement with service users and communities in a way that was previously hard to imagine in Northern Ireland.

This new social work qualification also aimed to achieve better forms of engagement more generally in all parts of the United Kingdom with social work clients through elevated expectations about the role that *service users and carers* would play in social work education at both strategic and operational levels.

The Social Work Degree – a New Era for User Involvement?

Levin, in referring to the degree in social work and the part that service users and carers would have in this, stated "… the thrust of all the new arrangements is that service users and carers get high quality social work services in terms of both processes and outcomes" (Levin 2004, p. 8). Levin perceived service user and carer involvement as being a key aspect of social work education which would see an enhanced role for such users in their positioning as "… active participants in service delivery rather than as passive recipients" (Levin 2004, p. 9).

The social work degree in Northern Ireland would also mirror this progressive thinking around user involvement which was occurring in other parts of the UK. In its *Rules for the Approval of the Degree in Social Work* (NISCC 2003) the NISCC, for example, stipulates the need for social work education providers to have:
- Mechanisms to ensure the formal and systematic participation of users and carers in the design, delivery and evaluation of course provision
- Policies on remuneration, induction, training and support to promote active user and carer participation in course provision
- Mechanisms to ensure user and carer feedback on agreed aspects of student performance. (NISCC 2003, p. 10).

The scene therefore seemed clearly established at various levels for incorporating the user/client perspective into social work education. What was not made so explicit however was how this important perspective may become portrayed within the social work education curriculum. Contrastingly however, detailed guidance was provided for educators to consider ways in which the *Northern Ireland Context* as a knowledge requirement could be managed within the curriculum.

This further validated and supported the rationale for undertaking research into this area to examine potential ways in which ordinary citizens could help social work students understand how experiences of living through conflict such as what had been occurring in Northern Ireland could impact on individuals and communities.

Service Users, Carers and Citizens

Many people in the service user movement in the UK prefer the term 'citizen' as more appropriately reflecting the egalitarian basis and principles surrounding their work (Beresford & Croft 1992; Rimmer & Harwood 2004). Although usage of the term may pose challenges for social work which has a history of seeing citizens as 'objects of assessment and prescription' (Rimmer & Harwood 2004, p. 313), perhaps the term can offer a departure from excluding the service user perspective in social work practice discourses.

The research upon which this presentation is based also uses the term citizen which forefronts the active social, political and civil rights of service users and carers, a position which challenges their perception as passive service recipients.

Citizen Involvement in Social Work Education
in the Northern Ireland Context

In order to investigate the potential for service users and carers to contribute to social work education, the author undertook research which involved consultations with representatives from all of the key interests in social work education in Northern Ireland.

Methodology

Four triangulation approaches were employed to investigate this area. Service users and carers were fully involved in the design of all of these research methods used for the study and in the subsequent analysis and presentation of findings.

A questionnaire collected views on various aspects of user involvement in social work education with particular emphasis on the part that users could play in helping students understand issues around discrimination. The questionnaire was administered to key informants in social work across Northern Ireland with representatives from social work training, social work students and social work managers, user-led groups and carer organisations. The total number of questionnaire responses was 85 (n=85).

A structured interview was also sent to a sample of 24 (n=24) individuals, including social work training managers, staff responsible for policy and other staff involved in post qualifying training. Respondents were asked to identify their thoughts on good practice in this field and how citizen trainers might contribute to the *Northern Ireland Context.*

Thirdly, a questionnaire was sent by email to a sample of social work practice teachers from across Northern Ireland. They were asked specifically for their views on the contribution of service users and carers around practice learning issues.

Finally, 13 user and carer-led groups and individuals were invited to *tell their own stories* describing their involvement in different aspects of social work education (n=13).

Findings

The following Themes emerged from the various methods of enquiry employed in this research:

1. The inclusion of service users and carers has an invaluable influence and benefit for social work training.
2. Service users and carers need support to train and educate social work students.
3. Service users and carers should be actively involved in the assessment of Practice Learning.
4. Service user and carer involvement in social work education should be grounded on social work values.
5. Service users and carers should be involved in all aspects of teaching, learning and assessment.
6. Service users and carers have an important strategic role to play in social work training in Northern Ireland.
7. Service users and carers have an important contribution to make to facilitate students in their understanding of the Northern Ireland Context (Duffy 2006).

The research suggested that some service users may already be well placed to engage in teaching social work students on issues around anti-oppressive practice generally given the proximity of their own experiences to being excluded. This point is clearly articulated in the following interview response: *"... the issues of discrimination they (service users) experience in their own lives, can be used purposively to enhance student learning"* (Interview Respondent). This comment resonates with Rimmer and Harwood's (2004) similar observations that issues concerning oppression were major contributory forces in the lives of service users.

Although the questionnaire responses indicated for many the unlikelihood of service users and carers being discriminated against in their role as trainers there were equally many observations which showed that discrimination was an issue:

"Service users come from oppressed groups and are likely to experience discrimination in all areas of their lives. I would expect this to be particularly the case in Northern Ireland where issues of prejudice and discrimination have never really been addressed either in the community at large or in social work education" (Questionnaire Respondent).

However another respondent had a different focus on the discriminatory issue which also needs to be examined in relation to the attitudes of some people towards users and carers: "being patronising in attitudes is another real form of discrimination" (Questionnaire Respondent). This has also been evidenced by the General Social Care Council (GSCC) review of service user involvement in social work programmes across the UK where it found that service users in their role as trainers often experienced patronising treatment by some social work students (GSCC 2004). A care experienced young person in this research also described experiencing such negative reactions in the training context when social work practice is criticised or challenged:

"Sometimes, people are particularly sensitive about any criticism of residential care and want to personalise the issue with the trainer."

Other commentators noted that principles of equality and inclusivity challenge service users and carers as educators to face the same parameters and guidelines as others presenters "Where they (citizen trainers) come across prejudice and/or discrimination directed at a group of which they are not members, they share the responsibility of us all to challenge the prejudice and/or discrimination in an effective way. Like everyone else they require training in how to do this" (Interview Respondent).

Having said this, there was a diversity of opinion about whether service users and carers, in their role as citizen trainers, should be involved in challenging prejudice in students or indeed in their own attitudes. Some respondents expressed the view that training citizens in this area would only *sanitise* and professionalize the service user/carer *reality perspective* that students would ultimately experience when on placement. There is however no evidence to support this position (Levin 2004).

The opposing view was expressed however by service user groups and individuals who thought that in their role as trainers they have a right to have the same awareness training on these issues as other social work lecturers would have, and therefore by not having the opportunity for *"awareness of our own issues"* (as one carer described it) such citizen trainers are not being treated as equals in their role as social work educators. The following interview quote is quite powerful on this point:

"Citizen trainers should expect to have access to courses and materials which will enhance their teaching skills. The alternative is to treat service users using the traditional approach which neither informs nor resources the skilled activity which education and training is. To do so would be a great disservice to citizen trainers and social work students" (Questionnaire Respondent).

Another comment however indicates that some users and carers already have the skills to deal with discrimination:

"Many service users and their groups are very well equipped to challenge student views on discrimination because they so often experience it" (Questionnaire Respondent). However, whilst the evidence does point to the value of expertise that service users can share based on experience, it must also be acknowledged that there is a degree of scepticism in the literature around "ordinary people taking on powerful roles" (Rimmer 1997, p. 33; Beresford & Croft 1992). Marmot and Wilkinson (1999), also urge us to reflect on the hopelessness and failure which the most unequal citizens experience which can lead to aggression and being withdrawn.

Nevertheless, in areas around discrimination, as in other areas, the responses for this particular study incorporate suggestions about how discrimination and discriminatory practice can be challenged. For example, there was quite a strong feeling that because carers and users already experience being out in the margins, that they will have the resources and strength to deal with such issues. A similar point is made by Rimmer and Harwood on the issue of service users challenging oppression "our work must challenge all forms of oppression whether by reason of race, gender, sexual orientation, age, class, disability or any other form of social differentiation ..." (Rimmer & Harwood 2004, p. 315).

The challenges inherent in this type of approach however should not be under-estimated, given that discussion on such emotive issues can often give rise to strain and discomfort in student interactions. To further strengthen and support the capacity of citizen trainers in this work, the findings from this study therefore recommend that training, awareness, and support structures also need to be put in place to inform, educate and help users and carers in this very difficult area around understanding and promoting anti-oppressive practice.

The Northern Ireland Context

Whilst the findings point to ways in which citizen trainers can respond to difficult and complex issues such as discrimination, there were also suggestions around specific ways in which service users and carers could contribute to students understanding of issues around Northern Ireland's conflict. The main point in this regard was the need to acknowledge the experience that service users and carers already have which should be explored as a way of helping students in their understanding of this area of knowledge. For example, it was suggested that carers may be in a position to share lived experiences, where appropriate, of caring responsibilities that have arisen as a direct consequence of 'The Troubles'. This could be in regard to caring for a relative who has been physically and emotionally traumatised as a result of being injured through violence.

In addition, issues around how the latter impacted on daily life could be captured by citizen trainers sharing direct experiences of how their choices in terms of service provision in a divided society were affected (for example choosing services in 'safe' geographical locations).

"Citizen Trainers could be supported to share direct experiences of how daily life and choices in terms of service provision in a divided society was affected, for example, by the geographical location of some services" (Interview Respondent).

It was also noted however that Service users and carers may need education and advice to support their involvement as trainers in this *Northern Ireland Context*, especially in terms of being aware of their own prejudices.

"It is 'okay' to hold certain views but service users/carers need to be aware of holding these views. It is not acceptable for these views to cause an adverse reaction. Training around awareness of our own issues may well address and prevent this" (Interview Respondent).

The next phase of this work is therefore focussing on developing a *Training Course* which citizen trainers can attend before they become involved in contributing to social work education. This should provide service users and carers involved with this work, the type of support that is needed in ensuring that this experience is positive for all parties concerned.

Conclusion

This small scale study endorses the value associated with service user and carer involvement in social work education in Northern Ireland. The evidence from this work strongly indicates that social work students can benefit from this perspective in virtually all aspects of their training. The work however has particularly focussed on the potential contribution that ordinary citizens can make in assisting social work students in Northern Ireland to understand how experiences of conflict affect individuals and communities. More broadly however there appears to be much merit associated with introducing this important experiential perspective from social work clients in the social work curriculum.

References

Beresford, P. & Croft, S. (1992): The Politics of Participation. Social Policy, 12, 20-44.

Campbell, J. & McColgan, M. (2001): Social Work in Northern Ireland. In: M. Payne & S. Shardlow (eds.), Social Work in the Western Isles of Europe, London.

CCETSW (1999): Getting Off the Fence.

CCETSW (1998): Social Work and Social Change in Northern Ireland.

DHSSPS (2003): Northern Ireland Framework Specification for the Degree in Social Work.

Duffy, J. (2006): Citizen Involvement in Social Work Education in the Northern Ireland Context, (http://www.scie.org.uk/publications/misc/citizeninvolvement.pdf).

Governments of UK and Ireland (1998): The Agreement. Northern Ireland Office.

Levin, E. (2004): Involving service users and carers in social work education. SCIE.

Marmot, N. & Wilkinson, G. (Eds.) (1999): The Social Determinants of Health, Oxford: University Press.

NISCC (2003): Rules for the Approval of the Degree in Social Work.

Pinkerton, J. & Campbell, J. (2002): Social Work and Social Justice in Northern Ireland. British Journal of Social Work, 32 (6), 723-737.

Rimmer, A. & Harwood, K. (2004): Citizen Participation in the Education and Training of Social Workers, Social Work Education, 23 (3), 309-323.

Smyth, M. & Campbell, J. (1996): Social Work, Sectarianism and Anti-Sectarian Practice in Northern Ireland. British Journal of Social Work, 26 (1), 77-92

Williamson, A. & Darby, J. (1978): Social Welfare Services. In: J. Darby & A. Williamson (eds.), Violence and the Social Services in Northern Ireland, London.

Theoretical References for the International Comparison of Institutionalized Forms of School Social Work

Christian Vogel

School social work is a field of social work which finds itself in different stages of institutionalization throughout the industrialized world (Huxtable & Blyth 2002). An overview on an international scale not only suggests that development processes follow different timetables in different countries, but also that there is great variety in the forms in which school social work is being institutionalized. In the international comparative perspective of the phenomenon, this can bring problems that we might not be aware of, since we intend to talk about more or less of the same "thing" when speaking of school social work in – let's say, Norway or the South of Italy. By this I do not mean that we tend to ignore the differences between national forms of school social work. On the contrary, I find that one of the most important motivations for looking beyond one's own boundaries and making comparisons is to learn about how it is handled elsewhere – this, of course, with the legitimate wish to learn how to deal with the related problems in a better way and to avoid mistakes. The difficulties I should like to mention lie in the approach to internationality and in the assumptions upon which it is based.

The sociological view of this topic shows immediately that, when examining school social work on an international scale, we are looking at a certain aspect of different societies. The institutionalization of school social work, therefore, has to be seen within the context of the respective society. In other words, school social work in society A is *not comparable* to school social work in society B.

1.   The Structural Analysis

1.1 Schools as Societal Institutions

The phenomena we are interested in are, as mentioned above, forms of institutionalization. Institutions can be seen sociologically as what we might call 'solutions to insolvable problems'. From a structural point of view, they are the result of the bundling of diverging societal functions. However, certain functions are on a manifest level, while other functions are kept latent. This ensures the attainment of divergent goals, at the same time maintaining the integrity of the institution as a whole. Successful institutionalizations are, therefore, stable arrangements between divergent functions that allow the handling of disruptive forces resulting from inconsistencies.

Schools have to be conceived of as complex societal institutions that combine a bunch of contradictory functions. At the top level, we can differentiate between the reproductive and the legitimation functions: Schools, on the one hand, ensure the reproduction of a given societal structure and, on the other hand, yield legitimacy to the structure. International comparisons should take in account that the schools' contributions to the functions of both reproduction and legitimation may differ considerably according to the respective stratification models. The same applies to the functions on a lower level, like qualification, selection, integration, and allocation (Fend 1980).

1.2 Differentiation Within the School's Inner Structure

A comparative perspective of school social work consequently needs to regard this issue as a specific institutionalization of the school in the respective society. This leads us to the relation between school and school social work. As with the relation between society and school, it is necessary to find a theoretical conception that allows us to vary the relevant parameters according to the specific social realities. I should like to refer here to my analysis of the institutionalization of social work in Switzerland, where I developed the hypothesis that in this country school social work is primarily the expression of a deficit in the school's legitimacy, which is in turn related to the legitimacy crisis of the state. I postulate that contradictions between the societal functions in the institutional framework of the school in Switzerland can no longer be successfully managed by its classical, scarcely differentiated structure. Tension tends to appear on the surface of the institution and there is no chance of working on it effectively. The reason for this is rooted in the rapidly growing inequalities in society (fortunes, incomes) in recent years. This leads to higher tension between the above-mentioned functions of reproduction and legitimacy. In order to ensure societal reproduction, the capacity of the school in generating more equality has been weakened. Reducing the social prestige of the teachers and installing hierarchies in schools lead to a lack of legitimacy for the institution. Though it may not be conceived of as such, this lack expresses itself clearly in a general feeling (both of the school staff and of actors outside the institution, like pupil's parents or other interested citizens) that the school needs support in terms of "the social domain". Along with this, we observe discourses on violence at school, immigrants and other social problems, as well as attempts to limit the teacher's tasks to core teaching activities and demanding specialized professional support for educational and other tasks conceived of as "social" (as opposed to "teaching" or "learning"). This leads to the institutionalization of school social work, which means it is thought of (on all sides) as *complementary* to teaching. As I observed in my research, school social work is often implicitly excluded from the framework of the school, which it aims to be part of. One big issue is consequently the cooperation between teachers and social workers. Many contributions to the discourse held by the professionals are therefore concerned with improving cooperation and trying to find out what organizational features promote or hinder "good cooperation".

If we apply the theoretical concepts, which I have sketched above, the observed cooperation issue presents itself from a different angle. Structurally speaking, the institutionalization of social work in schools creates a problem of integration. This means, on the one hand, the problem of limitation of the system and, on the other hand, the problem of establishing and maintaining an internal structure and the corresponding rules. Klaus Eder provided the basic typology of different modes of integration: Kinship *(Verwandtschaft)*, domination *(Herrschaft)*, and society *(Gesellschaft)* (cf. Eder 1977). Kinship integration is based on the simple dualism of belonging to a social unit or not belonging to it. The domination type of integration relies on an ordinal pattern that allows differentiation between elements that are near to the centre of power and those that are far from it. Societal integration, finally, dissolves the one-dimensional pattern in favour of multidimensionality: An element can be integrated to varying degrees in different dimensions. The dimension that yields the scale of integration becomes dependent on the task and the situation in which it has to be accomplished.

If we decide to conceptualize school as an institution containing divergent functions, the tasks that are to be accomplished vary in different situations. They cannot be organized according to a single function but contain the above-mentioned contradictions. The legitimacy of a school, or equally the legitimacy of school social work, depends on how these contradictions are handled. Any form of cooperation that aims merely to achieve clear distinction between the tasks of the different professions needs to fix the relevant dimension beforehand.

2. Empirical Evidence from a Case Study in a School in Switzerland

In a case study of a school in Switzerland (Vogel 2006), I found that the integration of school social work was attempted in the following way. A domination-type pattern prevailed in the effort to establish and maintain school social work. However, the available power resources were, in fact, too weak to accomplish integration (although the headmaster was completely in favour of this project). The analysis showed that there was a growing lack of legitimacy for any interventions by the school social workers and those on the teaching staff involved in cooperation.

Within the framework of field research, this study was based on the observation of interactions in a setting of institution analysis (Graf 1990). According to this, interactions are conceived of as containing a manifest and a latent level, which can be analyzed in terms of the institution. In other words, the institution is realized through the interactions taking place within its context. Therefore, such inter-actions contain information about the institution that generates them.

The theoretical framework linking the macro-societal structural perspective with the processes observable in the interactions at the micro-level consists of two components: The theory of symbolization by Alfred Lorenzer and the theory of communicative action by Jürgen Habermas. These two theoretical components are used to analyze interactions on different levels. The point of reference for both is the argumentatively saturated discourse *(argumentativ gesättigter Diskurs)* (Graf 1996, p. 186ff.). It is understood that the degree of saturation in a given discourse is higher when the participants' experiences relevant to the particular problem can be taken in account in the ongoing communication. So the saturation of a discourse is, other than in the Habermasian conception of the domination-free discourse *(herrschaftsfreier Diskurs)*, empirically noticeable.

The first obstacle to discursive saturation is the utterance itself. As long as nothing is uttered, obviously nothing can be contributed to the discourse in question. Once there is an utterance, it depends on whether the utterance is made in a symbolic or non-symbolic way. This analysis is provided by the theory of symbolization. Secondly, if an utterance takes on a symbolic form, it may be regarded as an argument and, thus, find its way into the process of communication. But even a symbolically uttered experience may not find its way into communication – in that case it does not take on the form of an argument.

3.   The Communication Analysis

3.1 Symbolizing – Desymbolizing and the Emergence of Clichés – Resymbolizing

With regard to the topic on hand, Alfred Lorenzer's main thesis (Lorenzer 1973) claims that language, or any other symbolic system, is not based on elements that are grouped in different ways, but on relations. The experience of a social relation with its concrete features provides the basic notion of a relation. Social constellations are lived as figures of interaction (*Interaktionsfiguren*) before they are tied to linguistic terms. Preceding this, there is a process of abstraction in which similar figures of interaction are categorized to what Lorenzer calls forms of interaction (*Interaktionsformen*). Forms of interaction are thus abstractions on a non-symbolic, and also therefore on a non-linguistic, level. They contain the whole range of qualitative aspects from past interactions and they structure future ones. In this respect, they are also referred to as *designs of behaviour*. A successful connection between a form of interaction and a linguistic term leads to a language game (*Sprachspiel*), where the form of interaction is linguistically represented.

With regard to our problem here, which evolves around the question of how to identify structural tensions within interaction processes, the important point is that these language games are not developed for every single form of interaction, nor do they last in every case once they are established. They are fragile arrangements. Language games can split up, leaving on the one side a form of interaction which is not linguistically represented. Lorenzer calls these *"clichés"*. On the other side, there remains an empty linguistic sign deprived of its symbolic: the desymbolized sign (*desymbolisiertes Zeichen*). Clichés keep their impact on behaviour, but they do not allow any reflection on it: behaviour is triggered without consciousness of the stimulus. Desymbolized signs, on the other hand, are unable to establish a basis for reflection on behaviour because they are no longer linked to the real proceedings in social life.

Forms of interaction develop in certain normative fields of given social contexts. (Socialization theory refers to these contexts as agencies of socialization: family, school etc.). In these social contexts, the designs of action are tied to symbolic representations *(symbolische Repräsentanzen)*. These representations allow us to consciously refer to the designs of action (for instance, in terms of "intentions", or "effects" etc.). In other words, only the symbolic makes it possible to *act,* as opposed to automatically *behaving* without consciousness and reflection.

The problem of desymbolization occurs only when there is a change between social contexts. The task to be achieved is to symbolize experiences that are related to the social context A in a different social context, B.

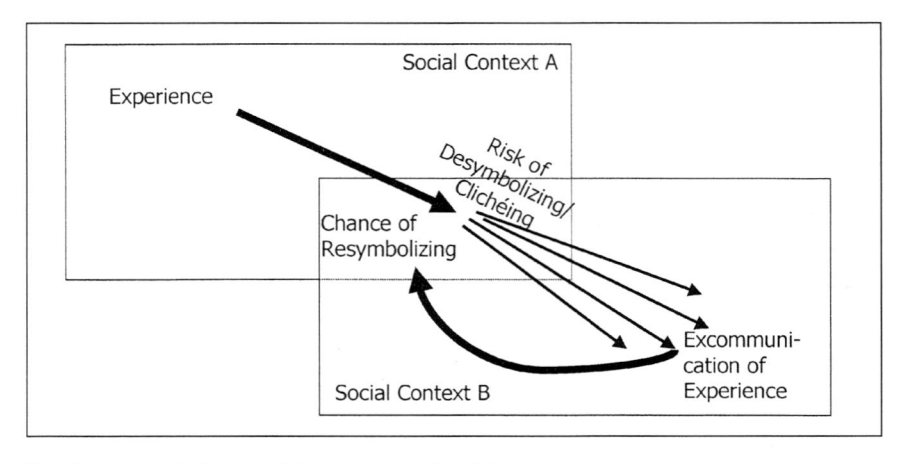

Fig. 1:   Desymbolizing and the evolution of clichés

Thus, we have to deal with processes of desymbolization and the development of clichés. Only by systematically referring to the original contexts can we (partly) reverse these processes: Apparently irrational reactions can be related to uncoupled designs of action. In these cases we talk of resymbolizations *(Resymbolisierungen)*.

Resymbolization processes can therefore cause saturation of a discourse if interaction is distorted by clichés.

The following sequence from a discussion between a headmaster and a school social worker may illustrate this:

Translation	Original transcription
H: Headmaster; S: School social worker	L: Schulleiter; S: Schulsozialarbeiter
H: I told the pupil p. he should contact you by today	*L.: dem [Schüler] p. habe ich gesagt, er soll bis heute mit dir Kontakt aufnehmen*
S.: m:hm [yes]	*S.: m:hm*
H.: I warned him, did he do anything?	*L.: sonst gibt es Krach ("susch räblet's"), hat er etwas gemacht?*
S.: h:mh [no]	*S.: h:mh*
H.: o.k., I will give him work for Wednesday afternoon [as a punishment; Wednesday afternoons are free for schoolchildren in Switzerland]	*L.: gut, dann gebe ich ihm einmal einen Mittwochnachmittag*
S.: (laughing)	*S.: (Lachen)*
H.: yes, I told him that	*L.: ja, ich habe ihm das gesagt*
S.: (laughing)	*S.: (Lachen)*
H.: and then-	*L.: und dann-*
S.: no seriously?	*S.: nein im Ernst?*
H.: yes, sure (...)	*L.: ja sicher (...)*
S.: no (rustling of papers)	*S.: nein (Rascheln)*
H.: he should finally come to his senses, he is a fool, or, what do you suggest?	*L.: der soll einmal zur Besinnung kommen, das ist ein Trottel ("huere Tschumpel"), oder, was schlägst denn du vor*
S.: if you don't see the social worker, yes, if you don't see the social worker, you get a Wednesday afternoon.	*S.: wenn man nicht zum Sozi geht, ja, wenn man nicht zum Sozi geht, gibt es einen Mittwochnachmittag.*

The headmaster informs the social worker that he has told the pupil to see him. At first the reaction of the social worker seems positive: He apparently agrees with the headmaster's way of proceeding. Then suddenly, when the latter says that he will punish the pupil if he doesn't obey, the social worker starts to laugh. He keeps on laughing when the headmaster confirms having threatened to punish the youth if he won't see the social worker. He behaves as if the headmaster is joking, which he in turn denies. It is obvious that the social worker does not agree, but (assumingly) he is just sorting out his papers.

The clichéd behaviour is first the laughing, then the sorting out of the papers. The link between the linguistic symbolic system and the social reality to which it is supposed to relate is disconnected. In our data, it is possible to discern the outcome of a process of desymbolization. In addition to this, we can also say something about the issue that has been deprived of symbolization: It is the divergence between the different attitudes towards the question of whether, and for what reasons, a pupil should be compelled to see the social worker.

3.2 Validity Claims and Communicative Action

The saturation of a discourse is not only reduced by symbolization problems but also by the difficulties that occur when linguistically represented contents are introduced into the communication process.

On a universalistic level, the problem of understanding can be described by the theory of validity claims (*Theorie der Geltungsansprüche*) (Habermas 1981a, 1981b). Understanding is based on the fact that the participants reciprocally make validity claims that can be accepted or contested. In our case, the following three validity claims are needed for the analysis: (1) The theoretical validity claim. This is related to the objective world of facts. We claim that what we say is true (propositional truth). (2) The practical validity claim. This is related to the social world of norms and rules. We claim that what we say is right, i.e. it respects the valid social rules (normative rightness). (3) The expressive validity claim. This is related to the inner psychic world of the actor. We claim that what we say is meant like that (subjective truthfulness).

In order to improve the degree of saturation, we can criticize any of these validity claims: "This is not true", "this is not right" and "this is a lie", respectively, are the three typical contestations. If the communication is not distorted, these criticisms can be used freely and sorted out in communicative action. Any limitation results in distortion of the communication and stems from an imbalance of power. We then talk about strategic action, manipulation or distorted communication. Communicative action is able to undo such distortions: a consensus about the facts can be reached in a theoretical discourse; a consensus about the valid social norms can be reached in a practical discourse; however, a consensus about truthfulness can only be reached by probation, i.e. there is no discourse but only the need to spend time with the participants (and establish a relationship of trust) in order to ascertain their truthfulness.

This concept of communication allows us to analyze interaction in respect to the use of language (*Sprachgebrauch*). Language can be used to state a fact, to establish an interpersonal relation and to express oneself. Hardly ever can these three aspects be sufficiently understood by what is linguistically "said" (propositional level of speech). An important proportion of the meaning can only be decoded by analyzing what is said within the framework of the given social context (illocutive level of speech).

With the help of these theoretical references, we are able to identify the degree to which saturation of communication is reduced by checking which validity claims are, in fact, fulfilled in the on-going interaction and which claims are not.

The following example may illustrate this:

S: School social worker; T.: Teacher	S.: Schulsozialarbeiter; I.: Lehrer
S.: well, perhaps we should again briefly describe the initial situation, well, yes [clearing of throat] I don't really know how it came to this discussion [coughing] you said you thought we should meet, didn't you?	*S.: also, vielleicht müssen wir nochmals ganz kurz die Ausgangslage beschreiben, also, ja [Räuspern] ich weiß gar nicht, wie es zu diesem Gespräch gekommen ist, [Husten] du hast gesagt, du möchtest gerne mit mir zusammensitzen, gell*
T.: m:hm, well it was actually a task from the parent-teacher conference, because certain parents there feel that .. ahm, well that some don't want to come to school and that certain people block each other and so and then we have just, [another teacher] Q and I have talked to them and {then	*I.: m:hm, also es war eigentlich ein Auftrag vom Elternabend her, weil dort einfach gewisse Eltern das Gefühl haben, dass äh, eben einige nicht mehr gerne zur Schule kommen und dass gewisse Leute da gegenseitig einander hemmen und so und dann haben wir, auf das hin haben wir dann gerade, [ein weiterer Lehrer] Q. und ich mit ihnen geredet und {dann*
S.: with} the pupils?	*S.: mit den} Schülern?*
T.: yes and afterwards (1) [teacher] Q. and I asked the class if they would agree to work with you again and that was actually the starting position when I contacted you, and now the point is simply that we give some feedback to the parents, to show that we have taken them seriously and that we have done something.	*I.: ja, und nachher hat (1) [Lehrer] Q. und ich die Klasse gefragt, ob sie nochmals bereit wäre, mit dir zusammen zu arbeiten und das war dann eigentlich die Ausgangs-lage, dass ich auf dich zugekommen bin, und jetzt ginge es einfach darum, dass man den Eltern ein Feedback gibt, nicht zuletzt auch, dass man sie ernst genommen hat und etwas gemacht hat.*

The social worker puts the following theoretical validity claim on the agenda: A description of the initial situation. (The clearing of the throat marks interference on the latent level, i.e. a symbolizing problem). Then the validity claim in question changes to the expressive issue, that is, the school social worker „didn't really know", which is immediately connected with the practical issue of „how it came to this discussion". After the interruption by the coughing, again a significant theoretical validity claim is raised on the manifest level: „you thought we should meet".

The issue is then raised as a practical one by the teacher: a task requested by the parents (... is the reason for this discussion, and not, as the social worker suggested, that the teacher thought they should meet). The teacher mentions the reason regarding the parents as a (manifest) theoretical validity claim with the practical implication that the parents are responsible.

He says that he has spoken to the class with a colleague and that the pupils would like to talk to the social worker. Again, with this claim of theoretical accuracy on the manifest level, the practical issue (on the latent level) is still being worked on. The question in the background is: what is the reason for the current meeting, or more precisely, who (the teacher? the social worker? the parents? the class?) is taking the responsibility for it. The actual problem itself, namely the situation in the class, is getting completely out of focus and, therefore, in the long run also out of hand. Finally, not the problem within the school is the main issue of the discussion, but rather the fulfilment of the parents' expectations. Better saturation of the discourse could now be reached by working on the latent issue, i.e. the specific responsibility of the school social worker and the teacher in the given situation.

4. Legitimation and Delegitimation Processes as a Reference for International Comparison

Lorenzer's theory of symbolization and Habermas' theory of communicative action allow us to analyze the matters that are excluded from the communication. In other words, we can identify the issues that are present in the interaction, but that do not find their way into the process of understanding.

If we look at school social work as a societal institution, then the fact that certain matters are kept on a latent level is not at all surprising. Institutions are agencies for the production of unconsciousness, as the psychoanalyst and social anthropologist, Mario Erdheim, pointed out (Erdheim 1982). Schools produce unconsciousness and thus contribute to the reproduction of societal structures. They slow down social change and are therefore referred to as a "cooling system" of society. This cooling process or – in terms of the micro-level processes of interaction – the exclusion of certain issues and arguments from communication leads to the risk of a lack of legitimation for the given institutional arrangement.

Max Weber's concept of legitimation is based on the empirical acceptance of social norms, no matter what the reason for this acceptance is. It may also rely on deception (*Legitimitätsglaube*). Improving communication involves, in this respect, taking the risk of destroying deceptions and of reducing the acceptance of the norms, which means nothing less than reducing the coherence of the institution. Institution analysis refers to these processes as "deinstitutionalization". This leads us to an apparently paradoxical result: School social work, which is institutionalized because of the school's lack of legitimation, *reduces* the acceptance of the institution if it manages to improve communication (i.e. by improving the saturation of the discourse by resymbolizing and introducing the issues into the discussion in the form of arguments).

The concept of legitimation developed by Habermas, however, postulates that substantial legitimation cannot merely rely on belief, but demands the reference of generalized interests. Communication, or to be more exact, the reintroduction of excluded matters into communication, is a means of raising the legitimacy of the decisions and interventions.

School social work, therefore, finds itself faced with a twofold legitimation problem: It has to gain and maintain acceptance for its institutionalization within the framework of school and, on the other hand, systematically risks calling into question that institution of which it has become part. This leads us back to our reflections about the types of integration: School social work may well be orientated towards a societal type of integration, but at the same time integration processes of other types are taking place.

An international comparison would have to examine the ratios and relations between the different types of integration. It would be interesting to see to what extent societal forms of integration occur and on which forms of integration the institutionalizations are based. The theoretical framework I have tried to outline here has the advantage that the micro-level processes of everyday interaction can be related to the structures we find on the macro-sociological level, making it suitable for international comparisons. Within this framework, different empirical approaches are possible. The analysis of interactions or more structurally orientated designs can be integrated, as well as combinations of the two.

References

Eder, K. (1977): Zum Problem der logischen Periodisierung von Produktionsweisen. Ein Beitrag einer evolutionstheoretischen Rekonstruktion des Historischen Materialismus. In: U. Jäggi & A. Honneth (eds.), Theorien des historischen Materialismus (pp. 501-523). Frankfurt am Main: Suhrkamp.

Erdheim, M. (1982): Die gesellschaftliche Produktion von Unbewusstheit. Eine Einführung in den ethnopsychoanalytischen Prozess. Frankfurt am Main: Suhrkamp.

Fend, H. (1980): Theorie der Schule. München: Urban und Schwarzenberg.

Graf, E. O. (1990): Forschung in der Sozialpädagogik. Ihre Objekte sind Subjekte. Luzern: Edition SZH.

Graf, M. (1996): Mündigkeit und soziale Anerkennung. Gesellschafts- und bildungstheoretische Begründungen sozialpädagogischen Handelns. Weinheim: Juventa.

Habermas, J. (1981a): Theorie des kommunikativen Handelns. Bd. 1. Frankfurt am Main: Suhrkamp.

Habermas, J. (1981b): Theorie des kommunikativen Handelns. Bd. 2. Frankfurt am Main: Suhrkamp.

Huxtable, M. & Blyth, E. (eds.) (2002): School Social Work Worldwide: NASW Press.

Lorenzer, A. (1973): Über den Gegenstand der Psychoanalyse oder: Sprache und Inter-
    aktion. Frankfurt am Main: Suhrkamp.
Vogel, Ch. (2006): Schulsozialarbeit. Eine institutionsanalytische Untersuchung von
    Kommunikation und Kooperation. Wiesbaden: VS Verlag für Sozialwissen-
    schaften.

Attitudes Concerning User Participation in Municipal Child Welfare Services

A Survey of Recent Graduates in Social Work and in Child Welfare Education

Harald Koht

Abstract

This article presents findings from a study of attitudes concerning user participation in municipal child welfare services. Recent graduates of programmes in
social work and in child welfare education from two university colleges in
Norway were questioned. By and large these recent graduates believe that children
and their parents should have a great deal of influence upon their own cases, but
they have reservations about the influence of user participation in the development
of child welfare services. These recent graduates are concerned about the impact
of user participation upon the relationship between users and their caseworkers.
An analysis of underlying factors appears to show that support for the ideal of user
self-determination is in conflict with intervention-oriented points of view. The
counter arguments favouring initiatives to protect the child at the expense of user
participation are more prevalent among child welfare educators than social
workers. This difference seems clearly related to the attention given to user
participation in the programmes of study.

Justifications for User Participation

Well developed arguments can be found for increased user participation in
political theory and in the literature of social work. Scholars often support
assertions that participation vitalises democracy and the right to be heard
contributes to safeguarding those who are affected by the decision-making
process. From educational and therapeutic points of view, user participation
contributes to processes that help users become engaged in and responsible for
their own treatment (Rønning & Solheim 1998; Taylor 2003). In the field of social

policy, user participation can play a part in contributing to better quality services for groups that are at risk (Taylor 2003). To a greater and greater degree these arguments are also made on behalf of children and adolescents. This is, in part, due to the increased recognition that children and adolescents have received for their competencies as social actors (Sinclair 2004).

Since user participation has always had a great deal of moral legitimacy, the ideological and professional arguments that are advanced to promote user participation can easily appear to be politically correct lip-service. As a consequence, a considerable gap now exists between the discourse of user participation and the practical problems encountered in its implementation (Kliksberg 2000). Professionals, who have reservations against the widespread practice of user participation, can be seen by opponents as being paternalistic and authoritarian. According to David Shemmings, one-sided perspectives in support of user participation lead to a clear polarisation of viewpoints among British social workers (Shemmings 2000). Those who support user participation favour user rights and stand in diametrical opposition to those who are intervention-oriented and who favour taking initiatives to protect children at the expense of user participation. Both groups are criticised for taking inflexible positions. Shemmings believes that this polarisation can be resolved if both parties pay more attention to situational factors. Rønning and Solheim elaborate this point of view by noting that "user participation can be implemented at different *levels,* that there are different *degrees* of user participation, and that user participation can be employed at different *phases* in an ongoing process"[1] (Rønning & Solheim 1998). This means that user participation in municipal child welfare services should vary depending upon the kind of decision to be made and the contextual circumstances that must be taken into account.

Research on Children and User Participation

In an article reviewing the comprehensive literature on the participation of children, Ruth Sinclair found only a few empirical studies by researchers who had been willing to undertake systematic evaluations. Nonetheless, the available studies appeared to support the idea that the participation of children had contributed to better services and to the personal development and social inclusion of users (Sinclair 2004). Norwegian research studies reveal that children have very little influence on child welfare investigations that concern themselves and their families (Oppedal 1999; Sandbæk 1999).

---

1   The author has italicised three words in this translated quotation.

Regarding parents, Norwegian research studies show that parents often experience powerlessness in their encounters with municipal child welfare services. Parents report that they do not feel that their concerns have been heard and that they feel excluded by child welfare authorities (Christiansen 1992; Sandbæk 2000). The control aspects of municipal child welfare services contribute to a reduction in the opportunities for partnership with parents (Bell 1999). Negative aspects related to the execution of powers affect child welfare initiatives for adolescents as well (Salisbury 2004).

Several studies examine how social workers view their relationships to users. In an American study of the behaviour of public servants, researchers found that social workers distinguished themselves favourably from other public servants by allowing users to have a great deal of say on how those social workers used their time (Brehm & Gates 1997, p. 129). As already mentioned, Shemmings (2000) found that social workers were polarised in their views concerning the participation of children in the provision of treatment; while some emphasised the rights of children, others were more concerned about rescuing children from difficult situations. Action-oriented researchers have been concerned to strengthen the appreciation of social workers for user participation by bringing users, including children, actively into educational programmes at the bachelor level (Boylan, Dalrymple & Ing 2000; Rimmer & Harwood 2004). Evaluations made of these initiatives underscore that users also need to have more information, instruction and a better understanding of their situation in order to participate effectively.

To conclude, these various studies show that even though many social workers and child welfare educators have a positive outlook towards user participation, many of the users themselves feel that in practice they have very little influence upon treatment plans.

Recent Graduates and User Participation

What are the attitudes concerning user participation that recent graduates have as they enter professional positions as social workers or child welfare educators? As a part of the project[2] entitled "User Participation and Professional Practice in

2   The research project is partially financed by the Norwegian Research Council programme for the development of knowledge in professional education and professional practice, project number 14306. Other project participants, Sissel Seim and Tor Slettebø, are acknowledged for their contributions to the questions under analysis and to the research report. Svein Alve (deceased) aided in the statistical analysis. The author thanks Frank Meyer, May-Britt Solem, and Lawrence Young for their helpful comments during the

Municipal Child Welfare Services", students who had recently completed their final examinations at Oslo University College or at Volda University College were questioned about the way in which they understood user participation and the kinds of influence that users should have. The questions were a part of a survey called StudData 2 carried out by the Centre for the Study of Professions at Oslo University College in 2001.[3] Some of the questions were asked of all graduating students who conceivably would be working with children (teachers, nurses, etc.), while other questions that specifically referred to municipal child welfare services were solely directed to graduating social workers, child welfare educators, and professional care providers for the mentally retarded. The answers from graduating social workers and child welfare educators are analysed in this article.[4] One may reasonably object that the data has been generated from professionals with very little practical experience. As a consequence, The Centre for the Study of Professions carried out another study in 2004, questioning the same people and using, for the most part, the same questions used in 2001. The findings from that study will be presented in a later article.

Professionals Comment upon the Influence of Users and Other Actors

The starting point for this study is that professionals working in municipal child welfare services have considerable autonomy in the practice of their profession, but that they also allow themselves to be influenced by other actors. In particular, the research team was interested to learn how social workers and child welfare educators emphasise the influence of children, adolescents, and parents, as individuals and collectively, through the activities of user organisations. The team wanted to compare the views concerning user participation and the understandings that graduating students have of their own influence and the influence of political authorities. In accordance with much of the research done in the work world, the study builds upon the evaluations that respondents themselves make and provide. The data is not objective, it is not based upon observations, and the information provided cannot be verified. As a consequence, we have no knowledge whether the evaluations provided by the respondents will be used when those same people are asked to make concrete decisions. The answers provided and the interpre-

---

preparation of the manuscript. A Norwegian version of this article was published in 2007 by *Uniped* 30, 24-35.

3   The data collection for the research undertaken by the Centre for the Study of Professions, in 2001, solely included materials collected from Oslo University College and Volda University College.

4   Phase 2 of StudData 2 was carried out in the spring of 2001. In all, 3067 questionnaires were mailed to graduating students and 70.2% of those questionnaires were completed and returned. The quality of the data is examined in a special documentation report (SPS 2003). A complete analysis of the data from the StudData studies made in 2000 and in 2001 has been made by Øivind Bergwitz (2002).

tations made can at best be seen as being helpful substitutes for data that a real situation at work might generate (Frank & Lewis 2004).

Respondents reveal opinions about user participation in Table 1. The table only reports the two highest scores (6 or 7) in a scale measuring the influence of user participation on a scale from 1 ("very low influence") to 7 ("very high influence"). The table shows that recently graduated social workers and child welfare educators overwhelmingly believe that the individual user should have a great deal of influence on the way in which his or her case is to be handled (80.4%). In fact, these recent graduates believe that users should have a greater influence over their own cases than the professionals who are responsible for decision-making. The same respondents believe that professionals should have greater influence in the development of services than users. Finally, respondents believe that organised groups should have more influence upon the range of services offered than the individual user.

Table 1:   Attitudes toward User Participation for Recent Graduates in Social Work and Child Welfare Education, 2001. Percentages Indicating "6" or "7" ("A great degree of influence") (N=245)

	Child Welfare Educators (N=114)	Social Workers (N=131)
Individual Users: Concerning services that are directly provided to him or her	75,5[***]	84,7***
Individual Users: Concerning the development of social services in general	42,3	54,7
Professionals: Direct influence over services provided to individual users	33,7	36,0
Professionals: General influence over the provision of social services	50,4	58,0
Organised Users: General influence over the provision of social services	40,5***	61,9***
Political Authorities: General influence over the provision of social services	25,7	26,1

Table notes: The questions asked were "What is your opinion of user participation? The term *user* means recipient of services in the public or the private sector, for example, clients and patients or pupils and parents. How much influence do you believe the following people or parties should have?"

*** Answers are significantly different for the two groups, p≤0.01 (Kolgorov-Smirnov test).

Respondents do not believe that the political authorities should have much influence in developing services in the fields of practice where they themselves work. Apparently, a potential alliance of professionals and user organisations should be allowed to form and develop social services. This view of the role of politicians may reflect a general scepticism toward authorities, or it may simply reflect the fact that respondents do not include politicians within the definition of "user" implied by the question. Comparisons between the two professional groups suggest that social workers are more supportive of user participation than are child welfare educators. The statistical analysis of the differences found show that these differences can, to a considerable degree, be seen as being random. However, the differences found between these two professional groups are statistically significant when a comparison is made between the numbers that believe both that the individual user should be able to exert a great deal of influence over his or her own case, and that organised users should have a great deal of influence upon the general development of child welfare services.[5] When compared to the child welfare workers, social work graduates believe that individual users and user organisations should have greater influence.

User Participation and the Influence Exerted by Authorities

The answers presented in Table 1 identify differences in opinions regarding how much influence different groups should have in individual cases and for the development of social services in general. However, this table does not help explain whether the differences of opinions among the recent graduates reflect a greater degree of emphasis upon user participation when compared to other forms of influence that can be ranked on the same scale, or whether respondents believe that various groups exert different kinds of influence. Since professional practitioners and politicians are not users, we might assume that when either of these groups has high scores in this study it is because respondents also acknowledge the legitimacy of other forms of influence, for example, influence that is based upon professional or political authority. A factor analysis makes it possible to test this assumption by charting the underlying dimensions and organising those dimensions into components (factors) that can then be treated statistically and thereafter interpreted.[6]

---

5   In order to determine whether the deviations are great enough to be statistically significant, the Kolmogorov-Smirnov test was applied to compare the two groups. This test is an appropriate one to use for comparisons between groups using ordinal scale measurements (Blalock & Hubert 1979, p. 266-269).

6   A factor analysis is based upon the assumption that the observed variables in Table 1 consist of linear combinations of a lesser number of underlying components or source variables (Kim & Mueller 1978, p. 8).

Table 2:   Analysis of Variance for Views on User Participation for Recent Graduates in Social Work and in Child Welfare Education. Values above 0.55 are in bold print. (N-245)

	Components (factors)	
	Factor 1 "Unconditional user participation"	Factor 2 "Influence of Authority"
Political authorities: Should have general influence	-0,068	**0,770**
Professionals: Should have general influence	0,362	**0,725**
Professionals: Should have direct influence on the services provided to individual users	0,091	**0,670**
Organised Users: Should have general influence	0,436	0,491
Individual Users: Should have direct influence upon services directed to themselves	**0,865**	0,156
Individual Users: Should have general influence upon the development of social services	**0,871**	0,032
Explained variation (%)	30,7	30,6

Extraction method: Major Component Analysis
Rotation method: Varimax with Kaiser-normalisation
KMO test: 0.684
Bartlett test of significance: 0.000

The results of a major component analysis of the answers to questions concerning user participation are shown in Table 2. The variables are the same as those shown in Table 1. The results show that two factors in particular explain a large part of the variations found for the six variables when these are seen together, but the two factors in themselves have different influences.[7] Factorial determinations that are higher than 0.55 (shown in bold print in the table) indicate that the variable being described has a higher factor loading and thus, it explains a greater part of the variations found. High scores for component 1 show a high influence of user participation for individual users in their own individual cases and for the general development of child welfare services. This component has been labelled "unconditional user participation". Component 2 is a common factor for variables

---

7   The factor analysis in tables 2 and 5 employ a varimax rotation and as a rule require that only factors with a value of 1.0 or more are included in the complete factor analysis. The analyses in both tables satisfy usual criteria in regards to the KMO test and Bartlett's test for sphericity. The numbers in bold print in the two tables show factor loadings that have higher values than those which are routinely used as a minimal requirement (0.55).

reflecting the influence of professional practitioners and political authorities. We have chosen to label this component the "influence of authority". Neither of these two factors is decisive for explaining the participation and influence stemming from organised users. The participation and influence exerted by organised users is moderately loaded by both of these two underlying factors.

When one views the results of the factor analysis together with the results shown in Table 1, one may conclude that in regards to the factor labelled "unconditional user participation," recent graduates in social work and in child welfare education prefer user participation by individuals seeking to influence their own cases rather than user participation that is directed at affecting child welfare services in general. On the other hand, when one evaluates the factor labelled the "influence of authority", one finds that the importance given to the work done by professional practitioners far outweighs the importance given to the work done by politicians, even when the development of child welfare services in general are under discussion. The importance given to the influence exerted by organised users can be explained by the fact that this ingredient is included in both components 1 and 2. In other words, support for organised users can be found in graduates that are "user-oriented" and in graduates that are "authority-oriented". This conclusion can be further tested by undertaking analyses that use the components in Table 2 as variables.

Does the Particular Educational Programme Influence Views about User Participation among Its Graduates?

A number of conditions might affect the view of user participation for an individual graduate in social work or in child welfare education. However, in this particular article I have limited the examination to characteristics found in specific educational programmes. What variable can be used to influence students to become "user-oriented"? This analysis assumes that specific characteristics of the particular educational programme can be used to explain a "user-orientation" in graduates. The hypothesis connects the particular educational institution, the particular course of study and whether or not user participation has been a theme within the educational programme.

Model:

User Orientation = Educational Institution + Course of Study + User Participation as a Theme within the Educational Programme

Since only two university colleges and two courses of study are included in this investigation, I have chosen to use these as dummy variables with a value of 0 and 1. User participation as a theme within the educational programme is evaluated on a scale that ranges from 1 to 7, and the answer "I don't know" is recoded and given the value of 4. "Unconditional user participation" is based upon the individual scores for component 1 in the factor analysis shown in Table 2. Since the dependent variable is scored on an interval scale, it is possible to make a regression analysis, even though the independent variables are not found at specific intervals. The model being tested has the following form:

Operational Model:

Component 1 = Oslo University College + The bachelor degree programme in social work + user participation as a theme within the educational programme

As expected, the analysis shows a low explained variation (R^2) because the model only consists of a few variables of importance for the respondent's view of user participation. Still, the model does show that the choice of educational institution, Oslo University College, best explains the individual respondent's positive support for increasing user participation. There is no significant difference in the findings between respondents from different courses of study, i.e. the social work programme or the programme in child welfare education. The subjective evaluation of a respondent concerning the emphasis placed upon user participation in the educational programme he or she attended appears to have had no effect.

Table 3: A Regression Analysis of the Educational Model (N=236)

Independent Variables	Dependent Variable: Component 1 "Unconditional User Participation"		Dependent Variable: Component 2 "Influence of Authority"	
	Non-standardized Coefficients B	Standard Error	Non-standardized Coefficients B	Standard Error
(Constant)	-0,311	0,205	-0,154	0,201
Oslo University College	0,356**	0,142	-0,028	0,140
Social Worker	-0,055	0,134	-0,363**	0,132
User Participation Emphasis in Education Progamme	0,052	0,038	0,073*	0,037

Component 1: $R^2 = 0.035$, adjusted $R^2 = 0.023$. $**p \leq 0.05$.
Component 2: $R^2 = 0.059$, adjusted $R^2 = 0.047$. $* p \leq 0.10$; $** p \leq 0.05$

A comparable analysis using component 2 "the influence of authority" as the dependent variable provides a different result which is shown in the right columns of Table 3. In this analysis, the respondent's course of study is the most significant variable and graduates of programmes in child welfare are the ones who primarily have high scores for being "authority oriented", since the coefficients for social work graduates in this table have a negative sign preceding them.

The conclusion to be drawn from these two analyses is that both the choice of educational institution and the choice of a course of study play a limited, but significant role for the standpoint that graduates take regarding user participation. It is not much of a leap to suggest that the differences found in the educational programmes can be used to clarify differences found in this study.

Arguments Recent Graduates Used to Justify Their Support for User Participation

Chris Argyris wrote about the relationship between the *expressed* theory and the theory that is actually *used* before undertaking decisions and actions (Argyris 1994). This study focuses solely upon the expressed theory or the arguments that recently graduated social workers and child welfare educators emphasise and express when they are asked to speak about user participation and the influence of professional practitioners. As a part of the StudData 2 study, graduating students at Oslo and Volda university colleges, in 2002, where asked to identify the benefits and costs they associated with user participation. The results of the survey questions are presented in Table 4.

Idealistic reasons for user participation have strong support among the recent graduates in social work and in child welfare education that have participated in this study. These reasons include the argument that participation in decision-making contributes to the development of responsibility amongst users (82.1%) and the argument that user participation is a democratic right (77.2%). In addition respondents provided more pragmatic reasons, such as the claim that user participation contributes to a climate of cooperation (67.4%), the claim that user participation leads to improved services (67.7%), or the matter of fact claim that the practice is required by law (43.2%). Arguments in opposition to user participation have very little support. All in all, the recent graduates in this study express strong support for user participation and justify that support by affirming both idealistic and pragmatic reasons for doing so.

Table 4:   Opinions Regarding the Benefits and Costs of User Participation among Recent Graduates in Social Work and in Child Welfare Education 2001. Percentages Selecting Alternative 6 or 7 ("Fully agree")[a] (N=289)

	Child Welfare Education	Social Work
User participation is a democratic right (human right).	75,6	78,6
User participation is a fundament of professional ethics.	59,7*	69,5*
User participation helps to engender responsibility in users.	78,3	85,5
User participation leads to better services.	62,3	72,5
User participation creates a more cooperative environment.	66,7	67,9
User participation is required by law and regulations.	33,7*	51,5*
User participation takes too much time.	10,6	3,9
Professional practitioners have better knowledge than users.	8,7	4,6
Users lack the knowledge to know what is in their own best interests.	5,3*	1,6*
User participation increases the level of conflict between users and service providers.	4,4	4,6
Professional practitioners should have autonomy when they practice their professions.	18,9	17,0
User participation is a theme that has received a lot of attention in the course of my studies.	20,0*	42,7*

Table notes: [a] The wording of the question was: "To what extent do you agree or disagree with regard to the following statements about the influence of users and professional practitioners?"

* Answers are significantly different for the two groups, $p \leq 0.05$ (Kolgorov-Smirnov test).

For most of the questions presented in Table 4, the differences between graduates from the two different courses of study are too small to have any real statistical importance. Only in three cases were the differences found large enough to be called statistically significant. The three cases concern; the role of users in professional ethics, the importance of rules and laws, and the assumption that users have enough insight to know what is in their own best interests. Child welfare workers had a lesser tendency to ground user participation in formal or ethical norms than did social workers.

There was one particularly marked difference between the two groups. Social work graduates identified user participation in far greater number as an educational theme that was given a great deal of attention in their own study programmes. This reflects clear differences in the two educational programmes. Although both of the study programmes aim at developing empathy in students and the ability to put oneself into user situations, social work students, according to the bachelor degree curriculum, have 100 pages of required readings on user participation, while students following the child welfare education curriculum have only 15 pages of required readings on that theme. It should be noted that the final variable identified in Table 4, strictly speaking is not an argument for or against user participation.

Eleven variables are incorporated into Table 4. One can ask the same questions here that were previously asked about the meaning of user participation. Perhaps these variables express two or more underlying factors? This article has already identified idealistic and pragmatic reasons for justifying support for user participation. In order to more fully investigate these matters, I have undertaken a factor analysis to identify underlying dimensions, and, if possible, to connect those dimensions to components that can be interpreted.

Table 5:   Analysis of Variance in the Opinions Regarding the Benefits and Costs of User Participation for Recent Graduates in Social Work and in Child Welfare Education. (N= 247)

	Components (factors)			
	1	2	3	4
Promotes Responsibility in Users	**0,852**	-0,126	0,016	0,068
Is a Democratic Right	**0,787**	-0,160	0,103	-0,006
Promotes Better Services	**0,773**	-0,162	-0,092	0,158
Promotes a Cooperative Climate	**0,749**	-0,014	-0,169	0,113
Is an Aspect of Professional Ethics	**0,676**	0,100	-0,016	-0,076
Is Required by Law and Regulation	0,456	0,115	-0,491	-0,279
(Is Questionable) because Users Lack Knowledge of Their Own Best Interests	-0,177	**0,741**	0,111	0,075
Takes Too Much Time	-0,037	**0,724**	0,200	0,043
(Is Questionable) because Professionals Have Better Knowledge than Users	0,008	**0,718**	-0,088	-0,041
Increases Conflict between Users and Service Providers	0,083	0,212	**0,818**	0,034
(Is Questionable) because Professionals Should Have Autonomy When Practicing Their Professions	0,012	0,124	0,191	**0,786**
Is an Educational Theme Receiving a Great Deal of Attention in the Study Progarmme	0,256	-0,073	-0,377	**0,605**
Explained Variation (%)	27,3	14,5	10,0	9,3

Method of Extraction: Major Component Analysis
Method of Rotation: Varimax with Kaiser-normalisation
KMO test: 0.804
Bartlett Test of Significance: 0.000

The factor analysis presented in Table 5 provides four components that influence their own set of variables, as is shown by the values written in bold print. For each of the variables, the factor loading is rather moderate. This includes, as expected, the question concerning the emphasis upon user participation in the educational programme, but, also, questions concerning the role of law, the role of conflict, and matters involving professional expertise. Most interesting is the correlation between the claim that "users don't know what is in their own best interests" and the claim that "user participation takes too much time". Obviously, spending a lot of time being engaged in user participation doesn't make very much sense for those who believe that users don't know what is in their own best interests. On the other hand, we must emphasise that these two opinions are not ones we ordinarily find among recent graduates in social work or child welfare education!

For understandable reasons, the components brought forth by factor analysis are not always given names by individual researchers (Lipsmeyer 2003). In this case, the first component is labelled "a democratic approach to user participation", while the second component is labelled "an authoritarian approach to user participation". "A professional approach to user participation" might be the phrase used to identify the fourth component, which only includes two variables.

The first five variables referred to in Table 5 contain component 1, which strongly supports user participation. It should be noted that the variable claiming that professionals should have a high degree of autonomy in their professional roles is heavily loaded by component 4. In other words, professional autonomy is not directly correlated with user participation. The dilemma between professional autonomy for social workers and the right to participate in decision-making for users of social services is a theme that is commonly referred to in the literature of social work (Sennet 2004). It is quite clear that the potential conflict between these two values is not dissolved during the course of one's professional education, even though professional autonomy, for the most part, refers to the ability to practice professional discretion. By and large, professional discretion is more directly challenged and can be quite difficult to maintain in the face of relentless economic and administrative directives.

Influence in Cases Brought to Municipal Child Welfare Authorities

In the section of the StudData 2 survey directed primarily to graduates in social work and child welfare education, respondents were asked additional questions concerning the amount of influence professional practitioners and users should have in the individual cases that are brought to the attention of municipal child welfare authorities. The starting point for these additional questions had to do with ownership. To what extent do users own their own problems during the various stages in the treatment process (Rønning & Solheim 1998, p. 41)?

The individual questions were specific enough in this section of the study to include 24 different variables. A ranking of those 24 variables by the recent graduates is presented in Table 6.

Table 6: Attitudes to User Participation and Professional Influence in Cases before Municipal Child Welfare Authorities for Recent Graduates in Social Work and in Child Welfare Education, 2001. Percentages for Respondents that Selected Alternative 6 or 7 ("A Great Deal of Influence") (N=245)

	Child Care Worker	Social Worker	Sum
Determining if a problem exists			
1 Adolescents	52,2	**69,9**	**60,7***
2 Parents	**54,8**	63,9	59,7
3 Professionals	47,8	44,2	45,9
4 Children under 12	20,3	37,4	29,5*
Determining what the problem is			
1 Adolescents	**64,3**	**71,4**	**68,0****
2 Parents	60,7	71,3	66,4
3 Professionals	50,1	40,7	45,0*
4 Children under 12	22,5	41,8	32,9**
Determining if something should be done			
1 Professionals	**63,7**	**55,1**	**59,2**
2 Parents	40,2	53,5	47,3
3 Adolescents	34,8	49,6	42,7**
4 Children under 12	10,6	24,2	17,9
Choosing between alternative forms of help			
1 Parents	**54,9**	**64,6**	**60,0**
2 Professionals	50,4	59,9	55,4
3 Adolescents	52,2	56,2	54,3
4 Children under 12	15,9	23,7	20,1*
Initiating, continuing or ending contact			
1 Professionals	**58,2**	**60,6**	**59,5**
2 Parents	36,4	50,4	43,9
3 Adolescents	28,8	41,0	35,3
4 Children under 12	11,7	19,6	16,0*
Changing the caseworker			
1 Parents	47,8	**57,3**	**52,8**
2 Professionals	**52,7**	45,2	48,7
3 Adolescents	42,4	51,2	47,1
4 Children under 12	21,3	31,2	26,5

Table notes: a) The question asked was (in English translation): "To what degree do you agree or disagree with the following statements concerning the influence of users and professional practitioners?" The answers for the two professional groups are significantly different with *p ≤ 0.1 and **p ≤ 0.05 (Kolmorgorov-Smirnov test).

The answers to these questions are rather uniform. Recent social work graduates particularly emphasise the decision-making rights of parents and adolescents in a host of questions that might arise in cases where parents themselves have contacted municipal child welfare authorities for help. Children under the age of 12 are not seen as having the right to participate in each and every matter requiring decision-making. When compared to recent social work graduates, recent graduates in child welfare education place less emphasis upon the user rights of children and adolescents. The differences are, in part, statistically significant.

Particularly in the beginning phases of treatment, when problems are identified and defined, users have a great degree of influence in decision-making. On the other hand, respondents believe that it is very important that professionals determine the initiatives that are to be put in place and the further contact with clients. The answers to these questions are particularly important because they concretise the meaning respondents give to user participation. The answers in this study mirror findings of a study of British social workers who distinguish between *children making decisions* and *children who are engaged in a decision-making process* (Shemmings 2000).

Conclusion

The results of this study show that social workers and child welfare educators who have recently graduated from professional educational programmes support user participation. They do so because of the democratic ideals involved in its practice and because users that participate in decision-making become more responsible. At the same time, both groups are concerned that professional autonomy can come into conflict with the ideals of user participation. User participation should be strengthened in the curricula for professional child welfare educators. Doing so will make it easier for candidates to become more conscious of the relationship between professional authority and user influence. Will the ideals of user participation be maintained when these recent graduates take their places in the practical work world and routinely encounter the everyday problems that are found in public service? That question can hopefully be answered by analysing the data from the follow-up studies.

References

Argyris, Ch. (1994): On Organizational Learning. Paperback edition. London: Blackwell.

Bell, M. (1999): Working in partnership in child protection: the conflicts. British Journal of Social Work 29, 437-455.

Bergwitz, Ø. (2002): Forventninger til — og vurderinger av utdanningen. Resultatet fra StudData-undersøkelsene i 2000 og 2001 for sosionom- og barnevernspedagogstudenter ved høgskolene i Oslo og Volda. Unpublished research paper. Oslo University College.

Blalock, Jr. & Hubert, M. (1979). Social Statistics. Revised 2. New York: McGraw-Hill.

Boylan, J., Dalrymple, J. & Ing, P. (2000): Let's do it! Advocacy, young people and social work education. Social Work Education, 19 (6), 553-563.

Brehm, J. & Gates, S. (1997): Working, shirking, and sabotage. Ann Arbor: University of Michigan Press.

Christiansen, C. (1992): Foreldreperspektiv på barnevernundersøkelsen. Nordisk sosialt arbeid, 3, 29-42.

Frank, S. A. & Lewis, G. B. (2004): Government employees: working hard or hardly working? American Review of Public Administration, 34 (1), 36-51.

Kim, J.-O. & Mueller, Ch.W. (1978): Introduction to factor analysis. I: Quantitative Applications in the Social Sciences, bind 13. Beverly Hills: Sage.

Kliksberg, B. (2000): Six unconventional theses about participation. International Review of Administrative Sciences, 66 (1), 161-174.

Lipsmeyer, Ch. S. (2003): Welfare and the discriminating public: evaluating entitlement attitudes in post-Communist Europe. Policy Studies Journal, 31 (4), 545-564.

Oppedal, M. (1999): Rettssikkerhet ved akutte vedtak etter barnevernloven. Oslo: Institute of public law, University of Oslo.

Rimmer, A. & Harwood, K. (2004): Citizen participation in the education and training of social workers. Social Work Education, 23 (3), 309-323.

Rønning, R. & Solheim, L. J. (1998): Hjelp på egne premisser? Om brukermedvirkning i velferdssektoren. Oslo: Universitetsforlaget.

Salisbury, J. (2004): Clients, claimants or learners? Exploring the joined-up working of New Deal for 18-24 year olds. Journal of Education Policy, 19 (1), 81-105.

Sandbæk, M. (1999): Children with problems: focusing on everyday life. Children & Society 13, 94-105.

Sandbæk, M. (2000): Foreldres vurdering av hjelpetjenester for barn. Tidsskrift for velferdsforskning, 3 (1), 31-44.

Sennet, R. (2004):. Respect in a world of inequality. Paperback edition. New York: W.W. Norton.

Shemmings, D. (2000): Professionals' attitudes to children's participation in decision-making: dichotomous accounts and doctrinal contests. Child and Family Social Work, 5 (3), 235-243.

Sinclair, R. (2004): Participation in practice: Making it meaningful, effective and sustainable. Children & Society 18, 106-118.

SPS. Dokumentasjonsrapport [html-fil]. Høgskolen i Oslo, Center for the study of professions, 6. March 2003 [Downloaded 27 September 2004]. http://www.hio.no/content/view/full/9171.

Taylor, M. (2003): Public policy in the community. Basingstoke: Palgrave Macmillan.

Foster Family as a Form of Family Children Care

Iwona Kijowska

Abstract

This article introduces the foster family as a form of care over abandoned or orphaned children in Poland. It also shows the way foster families are organized and appointed as well as the actions taken by The Polish Foster Parents Association. The result of their work is The Chart of the Rights of Children of Foster Families and The Chart of Basic Rights of Foster Parents, which state that all the actions about foster children should not be accidental and should take into consideration the holistic approach to a human being recognizing all his abilities and limitations.

> *To be a foster parent means to accept a rejected or orphaned by his/her biological parents child to your family. It means being the performer of a public task with the help of your own family.*
> (The Association for Foster Parenting, Elbląg Department)

Child – Parents – Family

Most often, the newborn child in a family is a great joy for the parents and other relatives. When the baby appears, the parents develop protective emotions, they learn to take the responsibility not only for themselves but also for the little, dependent on them, creature. It is also the time when they overcome the challenges that every new day brings to them. They encounter pleasant as well as strenuous moments. Unfortunately, not all the families handle those challenges. Both the structure and the functioning of the family can be then ruined. And this is the moment when the state or its social policy can help. "A family facing problems in fulfilling its duties and also a child from such a family is given help, mainly in a form of family guidance, therapy (…), social work and ensuring care and education for the child beyond the family." (The 12th March 2004 Act on social help, art. 74). Each family member would need such help but it is obvious that not everybody can and wants to benefit from it because of different reasons. Adults are not always eager to admit to themselves and others that it is them who need help. Therefore, very often they reject various forms of help offered them by institutions or private people, or show aggressive and demanding attitude, insisting on specific actions, i.e. financial support, when, on their side, they do not give anything in exchange. Thus, they remain in pathological relationships accusing "the whole world" of the situation. Obviously, children are those who suffer most. With no doubts the family, the closest environment for a child, is the place where the basis for the proper social functioning is formed. The time spent with the family can be metaphorically called "establishing the roots". What kind of roots do the children get if there are no parents at all or they are physically present but they do not participate directly in the process of transmitting the values that are essential for life and development? What if they do not fulfil their basic educational and care tasks? How can the child's personality be shaped if he/she gets from the parents such feedback as "you're the obstacle in my life plans", or "I don't need you", or "you're not important at all"… It has been noticed by many human personality researchers that family is the first place to satisfy basic needs. Abraham Maslow said, "the inborn human needs are organized into a hierarchy. Only when the lower order needs of physical and emotional well-being are satisfied are we concerned with the higher order needs. So, at the base of an imaginary pyramid we find a set of basic or "deficiency" needs – mostly physiological drives, whose end is the individual's immediate satisfaction. There follow, at a higher level, needs for safety, belongingness and love, and self-esteem." (Zimbardo & Ruch 1996, p. 404). The children and young people who do not experience suitable parental care should be given the opportunity to function properly by taking advantage of family care forms, day-care centres, and educational – care centres of interceptive form, family form (family children's homes, children's villages), or socializing and re-socializing form. Family care forms include adoptive family, foster family and protective family. The 72nd article of the 12th March 2004 Act on social assistance (The 12th March 2004 Act on social help, art. 72) says that it is the partial or total lack of parental care that is the reason of giving it to children by placing them in a foster family. Its task is to provide adequate living conditions as well as the conditions to relax and organize free time, proper psychophysical and social development, development of interests and abilities, and accomplishing all needs including the educational ones.

Foster Family

The possibility of taking care of children in a form of a foster family has been widely known for many years. Its beginnings in Poland go back to 1736 when the priest Gabriel Piotr Baudouin "founded a hospital for abandoned babies in Warsaw" (Walczak 2006). Feeding mothers employed by the care centre looked after the babies. Older children were taken under the care of villagers. Rev. G. P. Baudouin bothered also about the finances – he raised money from the charity (Badora 2005). A lot of changes in organizing children care have been observed since then. Both the political and socio-economical conditions have been decisive for introducing more or less institutional forms of care. Nowadays some modifications can be noticed. The Child Rights Spokesman (Kaczmarek 2004, p. 15) attentively monitors transforming the existing total care forms into family forms. It has been stated that no big centre can encourage close relationships between the children and the guardians. In children's homes with over 100 inhabitants it is actually impossible to treat children personally and individually. In such big institutions, very often called by children themselves "bidul" (a slang word derived from 'bieda' – poverty), their subjectivity is lost. There is no place for individual work with a child, which could encourage managing traumas coming from rejection and lack of love. Where is the time for just being with the child? If there is only one tutor for several children, and he/she is frequently changed because of unsteady staff, how can there be any emotional relationship between them? A relationship that will help to favour an open approach to the child's problems? It is definitely better to ensure conditions much more similar to those of a natural family. According to a social practitioner managing two social institutions and a foster father for many years, Paweł Urbanowicz, "a satisfactory foster family is much better than so called "good institutions of total care" (Urbanowicz 2004, p. 21). Another important change, as far as the legal and organizational matter is concerned, was the 1999 change of law referring to foster families. It transferred the department of children care from the Ministry of Education to the Ministry of Labour and Social Policy (Badora 2005, p. 275). It stimulated the widening of foster family duties. Now this kind of family is expected not only to care for the child but also to create a new environment until the abandoned child returns to his/her native family. Thus staying in that kind of a family is only temporary and lasts only up to the moment when the natural family's situation improves. Obviously, the family should be offered all kinds of help to make such an improvement possible.

Foster family is defined as "the form of total, temporary care for abandoned children who lack parental care, who, because of legal obstacles (parents were not deprived of parental rights) or age (older children) cannot be adopted. A family emerges when a couple or a single person undertakes the duties of upbringing not more than three children (in case of siblings the number can be bigger), assuming that between the person and the child there are not such legal results as it happens in case of adoption." (Kozdrowicz 1999, p. 242). The 12th of March 2004 Act on social assistance defines the types of foster families existing in Poland. These are:

connected to a child – where grandparents, older and grown up siblings or other relatives can become foster parents, *not-connected to a child* – trained strangers undertake the duties, and *professional not-connected to a child*, that is *numerous family* (not fewer than three, not more than six children; with exceptions for many children in a family when there can be more than six), *specialist* (including special needs children – and then not more than three children should be in such a family), *families of emergency character* (not more than three children for no longer than 12 months) (The 12th March 2004 Act on social help, art. 74). It can be seen clearly that the level of relationship and professional specialization is the criterion for defining the types of foster families. A different division is suggested by Urszula Kusio (1998, p. 22). She presents three types of foster families: *therapeutic* (in which children demand a special approach – medical and/or educational), *re-socializing* (in which children with special social needs or in danger of non-adjustment are brought up) and *pre-adoptive* (a family that accepts a child planning to adopt him/her in future). In this case the criterion of such division is the specialization in foster functions. It is important to consider the existing emotional relationship, the possibility of satisfying protective, physical and psychical needs when looking for a foster family for a child, as well as listening to his/her opinion of the family (from 13 years of age on, the agreement of a child should be decisive). According to Marek Andrzejewski (2004, p. 7) it should always be remembered that the main aim of placing a child in a foster family is his/her return to the natural family, in other words creating the opportunities to keep regular contacts with parents. Obviously, a parallel social work with child's natural parents should be conducted.

A foster family is granted help, both in finance and guidance form. The financial help is intended to support partial covering of the costs of living of each child. The amount and rules of allocating the funds are defined by the 12th of March 2004 Act mentioned before. The guidance on educational – foster matters is given by the people appointed by the local and state authority and social workers, educators and psychologists.

Foster Parents

Every time when a TV, radio or billboard advertisement calling for help in finding home for abandoned, orphaned or rejected children appears, the number of positive reactions rapidly increases. There still exists a myth that it is enough to give a child love, home and good living conditions to make him/her develop and return to a balanced state. This seems to be extremely deceptive. Such an impulse works for a short while only. Bringing up your own children is a very difficult task, whereas upbringing and care for the children of other parents is much more challenging. It is not only responsibility that is involved in such a task; it also demands readiness to accept various tasks, and very often the ability to react to unexpected situations. Children are not toys for adults. It is crucial not to let them experience another trauma connected with rejection. There obviously happen such situations when a foster family has to be terminated, but everything should be done to make it really a rare case. Therefore, one of the most important matters is the precise choice of foster parents and preparing them to fulfil the role they have undertaken. The rules for choosing foster parents should not be accidental. They are ordered by the social assistance Act already mentioned here. It establishes the institution that is in charge of organizing foster families, and that is the regional centre for family assistance. It can consign that duty to a public or non-public centre for adoption and care. In Elbląg it is the Non-Public Centre for Adoption and Care (NOA-O) working together with the Foster Parenting Association (SZR). The manager of the centre, Barbara Dębicka-Szumielska, and the psychologist, Małgorzata Jaskułowska, have worked out a special qualification procedure for the candidates for adoptive and foster families and those who want to run a family centre (Dębicka-Szumielska & Jaskułowska 2003). The qualification process is led in four stages:

The first – an informative talk. Together with the staff, the candidates for foster parents try to define what kind of family care they would like to carry on. They agree whether they want to be a foster or adoptive family, or run a family centre. In the course of the talk they are asked questions about their motivation for deciding to take care of a child, and about the system of social support they have or plan to have. Next, the staff informs the candidates about the qualification process and the conditions they should accomplish. At this stage they have to write and gather some additional documents which are required by the centre, i.e. application form, CVs written by their spouses, doctor's certificate of their health (stating that it is given specially for NOA-O), certificate of psychical health that states that no obstacles exist for them to act as an adoptive/foster family, an opinion from their workplace with a statement of their income, the copy of the marriage act, the couple's legal declaration proving a clean record, and the declaration of not being deprived of parental law. The authors of the procedure claim for themselves the right to terminate the procedure should there appear any reasons that could disqualify the candidates. This stage is closed with the agreement settling the diagnostic meetings.

The second – is the time when the material gathered previously is analysed. Special attention is paid to health, psychical, financial, legal and social abilities of the candidates.

The third – in which the candidates are thoroughly recognized during several diagnostic meetings (2 to 5). Different psychological and pedagogical methods and techniques are used at this stage – tests, observations, and interviews. According to the demands appointed by the 12th March 2004 Act (The 12th March 2004 Act on social help, art. 73) the candidates should guarantee the proper fulfilment of foster family duties. The correct choice is supported by various examinations of motivation, personal features, relationships in the family (clear marriage ties should ensure a stable relationship), educational and care abilities, readiness for challenges, abilities of identifying and understanding child's behaviour. It is also necessary to recognize if other family members will accept the child and if the candidates are fully aware of the family's actual possibilities as far as the foster family plans are concerned, including the system of support, organizing free time activities, the scheme of relationship in the family (natural children cannot become victims when new ones are accepted into the family, because it could ruin the relationship) and the age difference between natural and foster children. Foster parents should be the inhabitants of the Polish Republic, they should enjoy full civil and citizen rights. They should also take responsibility for the closest person or any other person if they have such a duty according to the law. It is necessary for them to have proper dwelling conditions and a stable source of income. At this stage the opinion of local social care centre is taken under consideration. Positive results of this stage promote next tasks of the qualification procedure. In Elbląg a training for foster families is organized, and after finishing it the candidates are given a certificate of qualification. The sample of such certificate is published in the Ministry of Labour and Social Policy instruction of 30th September 2005 (Dz.U. z dnia 19.X.2005, Rozporządzenie MPS z 30.IX.2005 w sprawie ośrodków adopcyjno-opiekuńczych). (In case of other Polish centres the training is interwoven into diagnostics, very often being its element and becoming a kind of verification diagnosis).

The qualifying procedure ends the *fourth stage* in which a session of a Qualifying Team of NOA-O takes place. The team consists of the centre staff: a lawyer, a psychologist, a pedagogue from an educational-care centre or institution interested in abandoned children, i.e.: MOPS (the municipal centre of social health), hospital (new-born children ward), children's home, psychological-pedagogical centre, family diagnostic-consultation centre. The future foster family is also invited to such a session. Only after having completed all those stages can the family take actual care of a child.

At this point that is the end of a qualification procedure. As soon as the child is placed in a foster family, it starts to fulfil its educational and care functions. At the same time a new phase starts for NOA-O – a phase of cooperation with the foster family. In the regulations of the centre and the association there are tasks that emphasize the constant improvement of the foster family. The Polish Foster Parents Association plays a significant role in this field. It is an organization that supports foster parents by arranging various local and all-Polish conferences, thematic trainings, and workshops developing educational abilities. *The Chart of Basic Rights of Foster Parents* is the most important achievement of this association. It says that "Foster parents are entitled to:

1. being treated with reliance and respect to their personal dignity and privacy.
2. being guaranteed confidentiality of information about the events happening in the foster family.
3. respect for their religion, beliefs, sex, origin, age, physical disability or state of health.
4. knowledge about the results of evaluation and feedback on the functions they perform.
5. being treated as equally important members of social workers' team.
6. being supported by the workers of courts and institutions that are in charge of helping the family and child.
7. being helped in preparing the child to gain independence and leave the family.
8. information about all social services and procedures that are involved in foster care.
9. trainings that can improve their educational and care abilities.
10. twenty-four-hour assistance in overcoming crisis situations.
11. co-deciding on the time that the child will spend at their house.
12. freedom to resign from their duties (in case they cannot handle) without any negative consequences on the side of social service and court workers.
13. keeping full freedom of decision about adoption, especially when the social and court workers insist on it and threaten to terminate the foster family.
14. participating in legal proceedings concerning the child.
15. getting all possible information about the child, especially if it could prevent endangering of the child's health or the safety of the foster family.
16. ensuring the safety of other family members" (Stowarzyszenie Zastę-pczego Rodzicielstwa 2004; www.rozterki.sylaba.pl).

The Chart of Rights indicates clearly that all the activities of foster parents should ensure responsible being with a child, liable professional work, that they should also comply with the state and abilities of parents in different moments of their lives. It emphasizes that it is better to retreat from unsatisfactory or enforced actions than to continue them against oneself. The authors of *The Chart* realize that a situation of strong frustration could initiate defence mechanisms and those could cause negative or disordered behaviour of both adults and children. Finally, the regulations in *The Chart* support foster parents in their educational and care actions, and they defend foster parents against all kinds of pressure on the side of the state administration or other people. It happens very often that problems are caused by natural parents who do not perceive foster parents as supportive to them but as enemies. They often express an opinion that it would be better if their children were in children's homes. Such attitude comes from their anxiety that the child will develop too close emotional relations with foster parents and, according to them, there is no such danger in children's homes. Thus, they confirm their immaturity: their own emotions and reasons are more important than the actual actions for the benefit of the child.

The concern for maintenance and keeping proper relations with the child's natural family is the main task of foster parents. One of the foster mothers described a situation when she managed to find the foster child's mother, father and grandparents, and she arranged some meetings of the family. The mother and the father lived separately, and each of them had a distinct and wicked life. Both were alcoholics. They were quite sober during the meetings but they did not show any interest in maintaining the contacts. The initiative was always on the side of foster parents and the children. Several meetings took place, a lot of telephone calls during which natural parents gave a lot of promises but none of them did ever come true. However, a great success of the foster family was getting in contact with the grandparents who had not been aware of the three grandchildren they had. Up till now they have had regular contacts with the children. In spite of the distance, they come to visit them at least once a year, and once a year the children go to visit them too, together with foster parents. It could be said that those children have found their "roots".

A Child in Foster Family

A child can be placed in a foster family on the basis of a court statement. In some exceptional cases when there is a need for quick action, it can be done "according to the parents' suggestion or agreement, on the basis of a civil-legal contract between the foster parents and the local governor. The governor has to inform the court about the contract." (The 12th March 2004 Act on social help, art. 72). The legal settlements regulate the position of children and the foster families. But nothing is said there about the emotional experiences of the children temporarily changing their situation. Magdalena and Przemysław Gąsiorek draw attention to the fact that such situation causes changes in children's behaviour and emotionality, which can be compared to those experienced by people who have lost some closest relatives (Gąsiorkowie 2004, p. 4). They undergo despair, then anger, apathy, sadness and resignation. After some time they seek help from others and then get interested in the environment and, finally, accept their situation which can promote re-organization of their lives. The inner conflict between the need of being loved and the feeling of revenge makes them suffer very much, weakens their immune systems, it can lead to depression an psychosomatic illnesses. To meet this exceptional situation of children the SZR has worked out *The Chart of the Rights of Children from Foster Families* which says: "Each adult member of the society has the moral and professional responsibility to secure care and development for the children of foster families. Each child in the foster family has the same rights as all the other children. Because of temporary or permanent separation or loss of parents and the rest of the family, these children need special means of help and conditions of development.

Each child in a foster family in entitled to:
1. being loved by his/her own family, especially when it needs help from social institutions; in case it is not possible – to emotional support in the foster family environment.
2. care and education in a foster family which was chosen according to individual needs of the child and can give him/her support needed to develop his/her potential.
3. being given help in understanding and acceptation of the reasons why his/her family could not take care of him/her, and support his/her self-esteem.
4. respect for privacy, intimacy and confidence of information concerning his/her life.
5. respect for uniqueness and development of the feeling of self-reliance and trust to others.
6. growing in respect for dignity and freedom, with people who understand, accept, respect and treat them friendly.
7. being given help in overcoming the effects of unfulfilled needs and negative results of early experiences (emotional, physical, intellectual, social and spiritual).
8. receiving preparation to social life and parenting, with the support of the foster family and other important adults.
9. receiving proper education, vocational training and support in choosing professional career (satisfying for the child and socially useful).
10. respect to his will when deciding on important life matters.
11. keeping contacts with the natural family and other important adults" (Stowarzyszenie Zastępczego Rodzicielstwa 2004; www.rozterki.sylaba.pl).

The authors of the chart emphasize that it is the emotional matters that should be taken under consideration in the process of upbringing children in foster families. Treating each member of a family subjectively will allow to achieve the most important value – a human being. They also stress that all the parts of the chart are complementary to each other and thus they should not be treated selectively. They are absolutely not just postulates (Gąsiorek 2004, p. 4-9). They describe the reality and they indicate some matters which are essential in working with children temporarily staying with foster families.

To sum up, I tried to draw attention to the recent actions in Poland connected with foster parenting. You can thus notice:
1. The trends of transforming the care for abandoned and orphaned children from institutional forms (children's homes) into family forms (foster or adoptive families).
2. Appointing and proper organization of foster families stated by the 12th March 2004 Act on social assistance, and ministry instructions. They make the basis for legal actions, and give the possibilities of working out other attitudes connected with qualification procedures and preparing the candidates for fulfilling the tasks.
3. The actions of SZR are especially valuable. Creating *The Chart of the Rights of Children from Foster Families* and *The Chart of Basic Rights of Foster Parents* indicates that the actions in families cannot be accidental and they are connected with the holistic approach to a human being (seeing his/her abilities and limitations), that they should be directed and realized with great responsibility.

We can notice that more and more actions are taken in our country to encourage foster parenting. The idea of creating foster families is widely promoted. However, there is still too little information about their functioning, especially about the functioning of the children in foster families and the possibilities of solving their problems. It happens quite often that foster parents resign. The difficulties in communication, little knowledge about children development, conflicts, financial problems, lack of support and understanding are only some reasons of retreating. The lack of systematic cooperation of scientists, psychologists and pedagogues, media and organizations leading social actions, in showing the actual state of foster family is unquestionable (Gąsiorek 2007; www.rozterki.sylaba.pl/wychowanie/psych 11-12). Therefore it is necessary to modify the way of presenting, but also thinking about foster parenting in the society, and to show the perspectives for abandoned or orphaned children.

References

Andrzejewski, M. (2004): Nierespektowane prawo. Rodziny zastępcze w orzecznictwie Trybunału Strasburskiego, in: *Rozterki Wychowawcze*. *Pismo rodziców i opiekunów Stowarzyszenia Zastępczego Rodzicielstwa, 1* (15),

Badora, S. (2005): Rodzina zastępcza. In: J. Brągiel & S. Badora (eds.), Formy opieki, wychowania i wsparcia w zreformowanym systemie społecznym, Wydawnictwo Uniwersytetu Opolskiego, Opole, p. 272-287.

Dębicka-Szumielska, B. & Jaskułowska, M. (2003): Proces kwalifikacji kandydatów na rodziny adopcyjne, zastępcze i prowadzące placówkę rodzinną. Materiały do użytku wewnętrznego (udostępnione przez autorki).

Dz. U. z dnia 12.III. 2004, No 64, Act on social help.

Dz. U. z dnia 19.X.2005, Rozporządzenie MPS z 30.IX.2005 w sprawie ośrodków adopcyjno-opiekuńczych.

Gąsiorek, M. (2007): Dlaczego rodzice zastępczy w Polsce rezygnują ze swych funkcji? Próba interpretacji problemu na podstawie odpowiedzi rodziców zastępczych; www.rozterki.sylaba.pl/wychowanie/psych 11-12.

Gąsiorek, P. (2004): Nowe prawo cz. II. Karta praw dzieci z rodzin zastępczych, in: *Rozterki Wychowawcze. Pismo rodziców i opiekunów Stowarzyszenia Zastępczego Rodzicielstwa, 3/4* (17-18), p. 4-9

Gąsiorkowie M., P. (2004): Adopcja czy rodzina zastępcza? Dylemat prawno-opiekuńczy – czyli o „dziecku wylanym z kąpielą", in: *Rozterki Wychowawcze. Pismo rodziców i opiekunów Stowarzyszenia Zastępczego Rodzicielstwa, 1* (15), p .4

Kaczmarek, M. (2004): Od placówek do rodzinnej opieki nad dzieckiem. Uwagi i wnioski rzecznika Praw Dziecka do dotychczasowych działań samorządów., in: *Rozterki Wychowawcze. Pismo rodziców i opiekunów Stowarzyszenia Zastępczego Rodzicielstwa, 3/4* (17-18), p. 15.

Kozdrowicz, E. (1999): Rodzina zastępcza, in: Lalk, D. & Pilch, T. (eds.) Elementarne pojęcia pedagogiki społecznej i pracy socjalnej, Wydawnictwo Akademickie „Żak", Warsaw, p. 242

Kusio, U. (1998): Rodzina zastępcza jako środowisko wychowawcze. Studium socjologiczne na przykładzie Lublina, Wydawnictwo Uniwersytetu M. C. Skłodowskiej, Lublin, p. 22

Stowarzyszenie Zastępczego Rodzicielstwa (2004): Karta Praw Dzieci z Rodzin Zastępczych, Artykuł dofinansowany z Fundacji im S. Batorego; (http://www.rozterki.sylaba.pl z dnia 7.01.2007).

Urbanowicz, P. (2004): Rodzicielstwo zastępcze dzisiaj. Wystąpienie z konferencji „Przeciw porzuceniu – rodzice zastępczy nadzieją", in: *Rozterki Wychowawcze. Pismo rodziców i opiekunów Stowarzyszenia Zastępczego Rodzicielstwa, 3-4* (17-18), 21.

Walczak, M. (2006): Rodzina zastępcza jako środowisko wychowawcze – charakterystyka i funkcjonowanie na przykładzie rodzin zastępczych w Zduńskiej Woli, in: Krzyszkowski, J. & Majer, R. (eds.) Pomoc społeczne rodzinie – z warsztatów praktyków. Rodziny zastępcze. Opieka środowiskowa. Centrum AV, Częstochowa.

Zimbardo, P.G. & Ruch, F.L. (1996): Psychology and life. Wydawnictwo Naukowe PWN, Warsaw, p. 404.

Social Workers at Schools
Defining Conditions for Effective Help in Solving Students' Problems

Irena Sorokosz

Almost in all aspects of social life there are many unexpected changes, which obligates the way we solve and handle with different situations and problems. It's concerned with the way we learn and absorb information. It's also connected with stress and pressure we experience everyday. Unfortunately, there are people who can't solve problems on their own. We are obligated to help them with their difficult situations, stress, pressure, crisis and hardships. In this way we create a new model of social work. It's connected with an increase and adding a new form of help (www.wshe.pl/2007-02-02, Mielczarek).

Basic definition of social work in Poland says that "social work is a professional activity oriented to help people and their families to support or recover an ability to be functional in society" (Ustawa o pomocy społecznej 1993, p. 5). Social work is also associated with giving certain values such as:
- undertaking activities which ensure social well-being
- improvement of living conditions for individuals, families and groups of people
- undertaking activities which promote social justice (PASW Code of Ethics).

PASW Code of Ethics Social Workers refers to the idea of social work – respecting human's dignity and protecting that dignity, respecting human's right to self-determination, ensuring and caring of equal opportunities.

Social work takes different forms such as: (1) rescuing (in crisis situations), (2) care, (3) helping (supporting development), (4) social compensation (compensating of defects) (Radlińska 1961). They also include various forms of counselling, for example: law, family, psychology, pedagogy counselling or help in solving difficult life's problems (Firlit-Fesnak & Szatur-Jaworska 1995). Counselling is defined as modern core of social work because when it is given early enough, such pieces of advice are a form of prevention at the same time (www.wshe.pl/2007-02-02, Mielczarek). Counselling plays a significant role when it comes to children and young people.

The learning period is a time of intensive changes in intellectual, psychical and social areas. Moulding of students' personalities and characters goes hand in hand with development of values, social norms and patterns of behaviour. On the other hand, young people put a lot of effort into dealing with educational tasks and living up to school's expectations. In recent years, we have been observing a permanent increase in a number of students with school difficulties, problems ranging from homesickness, anxiety, eating disorders or suicidal thoughts. On each level of school: primary, middle or high school there are students who need help, support or counselling.

History of counselling in Poland dates from 19th to 20th century (Kozdrowicz 1995). At first, counselling was concentrated on giving advice how to choose an occupation and cope with career problems. The first careers office was established in 1907. As counselling developed in other countries, in Poland there also began to notice various problems like nervous disorders and behavioural problems among difficult children.

From the 1927 to 1930 counselling and guidance service were established whose primary task was to assess and select children with mental handicap. Around 1958 there were established first typical school counselling which were called educational counselling. They were established because of the increase of problems in behaviour towards teachers, peer groups, parents and elderly people. A few years later (1964) the minister of education made a suggestion to combine career and educational counselling. Since 1964 counselling service for young people, teachers and parents has been called Psychology and Pedagogy Guidance (Poradnie Psychologiczno-Pedagogiczne).

In Poland there are 557 PPP and 21 specialist counselling service in which psychologists, pedagogues, speech therapists, remedial teachers and social workers are engaged. Since 1975 at many schools, additionally are employed workers who could help schools on psychosocial issues. They play the same role as school social workers in the USA (www.sswaa.org/members/resolutions/ training.thtml/2007-01-18), Great Britain (www.basw.co.uk/2007-03-02) or Canada (www.casw-acts.ca/practice/schoolsocialworker.htm/2007-03-02), but in Poland they are called school pedagogues. The pedagogue is required to obtain master degree. Since they provide specialised services at schools it is recommended that they must be certificated in psychology, pedagogy or sociology.

They are employed as a teacher but they don't teach, and don't have their own class. Pedagogues at schools have a broad scope/range of responsibilities. They work as social workers, counsellors, educators, mediators, negotiators, sometimes as career consultants.

They use their understanding of various interacting impacts of school, home and community in assessing students needs, providing training and educational programs or serving as advocates for students.

School pedagogues take care of students at school and outside school and coordinate interaction with students' families (Trojan 2006). They provide a vital link among school, home and community. A good side of such a solution is that a school pedagogues or psychologist constantly participates in school life. He/she has a better understanding of the unique school environment, which makes their work more effective. On the other hand, this solution has also a negative side.

Main directions of their work at school are: prevention, diagnostic tests and therapy. According to a directive of the minister of education psychology and pedagogy counselling lies in (Rozporządzenie Ministra Edukacji i Sportu 2003):
1. assessing children's environment;
2. evaluating students' potential abilities and individual needs of students and recognising possibility of their fulfilment;
3. identifying reasons for difficulties in learning and recognising why some students are not successful in school ;
4. supporting highly gifted students;
5. organising various forms of aid and minimizing effects of developmental disabilities;
6. organising special education for students with physical, mental, social, emotional or other educational disabilities;
7. introducing prevention programs and educational programs;
8. promoting healthy lifestyle, conducting training programs for students, teachers and parents;
9. conducting career monitoring programs and supporting students' choice of an occupation or a vocational school;
10. supporting carers, parents and teachers in solving educational problems;
11. mediating between sides of crisis, crisis interventions.

A school pedagogue employ appropriate work methods in situations happening within students' educational process. Those are individual or grouping methods.

Direct Services with students deal with:
- Conducting assessment of students' needs
- Reporting suspected child abuse/neglect
- Promoting safe and caring schools
- Promoting regular school attendance and coordinating drop out prevention programs
- Participating in the development of behavioural modification plans
- Providing short/long-term case management services to individual students
- Providing training and educational or prevention programs
- Providing individual counselling and crisis intervention services
- Completing social developmental case studies
- Referrals to community agencies
- Coordination of services with community agencies.

The basic problems which students come for help are: (1) specific learning disabilities (dyslexia), (2) behavioural problems such as accessing anger, acting out, eating disorders, aggressive behaviour, suicidal behaviour, drug and alcohol abuse, violence or bulling, truancy, (3) emotional issues such as episodes of sadness or depression, mood swings, anger managing, poor self-esteem, coping with stress such as homework, test anxiety or phobias, (4) social withdrawal or isolation, peer pressure.

In addition to counselling service, a school pedagogue is also engaged in education and prevention actives as well as activities designed to create a more caring and emotionally responsive environment. They also conduct workshops and give classroom presentations for students on topics such as stress management, coping with difficult situations, depression, relationship and communication.

Within Direct Services with Families a school pedagogue employs appropriate social work methods to assure students' positive academic and social outcomes.
- Promoting parental responsibility for regular school attendance
- Conducting family needs assessments
- Providing crisis intervention services
- Training of parenting skills
- Educating parent how to cope with special children's needs and child abuse
- Assisting families with the interpretation of school policies and procedures.

Direct Services with teachers or school personnel deal with:
- Arranging meetings
- Organising workshops of interpersonal skills
- Providing individual counselling and brief interventions
- Giving support in identifying and considering solutions to problems

- Solving conflicts between teachers and students or conflicts between students
- Conducting lectures which concern students' different problems.

A considerable increase of unemployment and poverty of many families has caused that in recent years many activities of a school pedagogue are connected with other social organisations, for instance:
- Municipal Social Welfare Centre
- Centre of Social Policy
- State Fund for Rehabilitation of Disabled People (PFRON)
- Psychology and Pedagogy Guidance.

The main tasks of a pedagogue in this field are: (1) having charge of scholarship fund and maintenance grant, (2) providing school lunch programme within the school area, (3) organising holiday trips, students' leisure time and rest, (4) organising material help.

Cooperation also concerns estimating children's needs, determining an effective form of help given to children and their families as well as monitoring this help.

The role of a school pedagogue in the system of education in Polish:

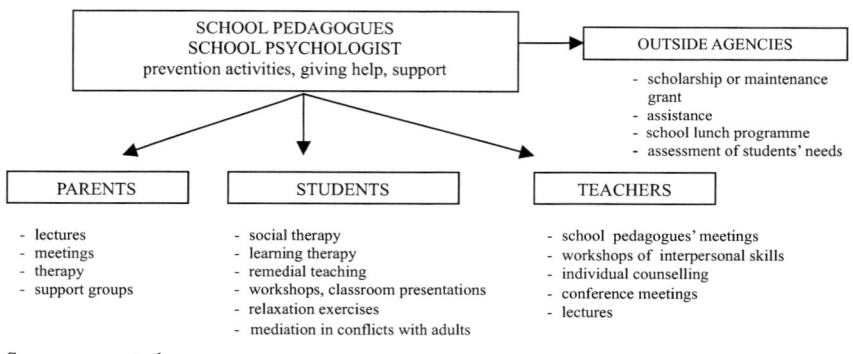

Source: own study

Work of a school pedagogue is greatly needed and useful but only if there are vividly established rules and standards, one may carry out his job at school effectively.

Professional help demands theoretical knowledge and an ability of creative thinking, communicating and solving problems and conflicts (Nocuń &

Szmagalski 1998). This profession also involves acting in accordance with job rules that include particular standards of ethical conducts (Kodeks etyczno-zawodowy psychologa 2005). The main value for a psychologist is the other person's sake. The aim of his/her professional activities is giving help to other people in solving their lives' hardships, achieving a better quality of life by the means of development of individual abilities and the improvement of human relationships (Strelau 2000).

In practice it might be observed that the professional role of a pedagogues depends not only on themselves but also on headmasters, teaching staff and students. We can distinguish several roles typical for school pedagogues (Sałasiński & Badziukiewicz 2003):

1. 'The third manager' – a very huge meaning if this position was achieved on the way of recognition, accomplishments and accepting the value of work done.
2. 'A man who puts out the fire' – such a person doesn't take part in everyday planning or accomplishing current matters but if something goes wrong ('burns') such a pedagogue acts effectively. If such urgent cases are rare there appears a danger of falling into routine. On the contrary, if such cases are too frequent, it might result in chaos, stress and acting under time pressure.
3. 'A policeman' – such an employee is a law executor, regulations guardian or an investigator. A student is under an impression that he was sent to a psychologist or pedagogue as a punishment or under a must. Sometimes a pedagogue conducts an investigation that is to explain some issues, punish the guilty or to discover drugs within school area.
4. 'A person to everything' – it is a person who undertakes every task: a duty in a reception desk, replacing other teacher, writing different programmes, reports and filling in school documents, conducting meetings with parents, students and teachers. One has to possess much strength and time to fulfil so many tasks.
5. 'A bosom friend' – this type might be usually met among young employees; such a position might result in the loss of the distance needed to assess a situation. Emerging emotional bounds additionally disrupt the ability of diagnosing and helping. A school psychologist and pedagogue cannot be a pal, above all he/she is an adult who might help.
6. 'A jobsworth' – it may be said that this type is the embodiment of set of rules. He/she doesn't connect his/her doings with problems but with formal rules that are compulsory at school. This role is sometimes connected with a role of a pedagogue-bureaucrat who is more interested in documents than in students' problems. Such a person doesn't often have time to help since he/she guards documents.

Those are only a few professional roles that can be observed at school. Fortunately, majority of pedagogues are able to create conditions to giving help effectively. They must be friendly and trustworthy so that everybody would like to talk to him/her honestly. Among many qualities such ones are essential: sensitivity to other people's problems, empathy, objectivity, responsibility for one's words, trustworthiness and being frank (Sajdak 2005).

An effective help for students is dependent on such attitudes as: acceptation, respect for a student and honesty, confidentiality and being responsive to the needs of both family and students. The basic abilities of pedagogues are: being able to provide interventions and removing systemic, environmental, family, physical or emotional barriers to learning.

L.M. Brammer shows a role of qualities of personality in such a way (Czajkowska & Nauczyciel 1999):

HELPER'S PERSONALITY +	ABILITIES	= CONDITIONS THAT ENABLE DEVELOPMENT
QUALITIES	UNDERSTANDING	TRUST
ATTITUDES	CREATING COMFORT	RESPECT
VALUES	ACTIONS	FREEDOM

Source: Czajkowska & Nauczyciel 1999, p. 550.

Experiment shows that subjective treatment of a student, kindliness but most of all ability of listening to are a half of the success. A young man who needs support, showing the way or help counts on honest and solid information. He/she doesn't expect preaching, is afraid of assessment or critics. A pedagogue doesn't impose his/her way of thinking or understanding (King 2003). He/she doesn't try to persuade an interlocutor to change his/her opinions or acting. Instead of forming prohibitions or giving advice, he/she tries to broaden his/her interlocutor's knowledge of the person's actions or rather their consequences and of many other possibilities of acting (Kozłowski 1996).

To help effectively one has to fulfil several conditions, which is quite difficult, especially for psychologists who work as pedagogue at school. Many of them talk about a dilemma of being between a student and a teacher to say it in a different way: being caught between the devil and the deep blue sea. They should always support a student, but not always is that so easy and obvious. Working in every profession, except for doing one's own duties, whether one wants or not, friendships, relationships are formed between people. A school psychologist on this account is surely closer to teachers rather than to students (www. psychologia.net.pl/artykul.php/2007-02-14, Maciejewska).

When starting work, therapy with some person, every psychologist starts from establishing a therapy agreement that consists of their establishments for a therapy. At school it is often imposed: 'something has to be done with him as one cannot stand such behaviour during a lesson', 'this child has to be quieten', 'he should meet the psychologist constantly', etc.

When a student presents behaviour that cannot be accepted and makes it difficult for a teacher to conduct a lesson then such a pupil should be taken under a psychologist's help in accordance with school procedures (and also with parents' agreement). Such a student often avoids a psychologist. When he comes to a psychologist's office, he shows all well-known methods of resistance.

For some groups of students that are threatened with a psychologist, they are perceived in negative, war categories; perceived as a person who is an ally of teachers. Unfortunately, this way of thinking can be as well noticed among parents. Parents don't come to a psychologist for help, what is more they don't expect any help, they are satisfied with their *status quo*; they come because a teacher told them to do so, they only fulfil their parental responsibility towards school.

Then, another problem a psychologist has to face is the embarrassment that is connected with entering his/her room. Despite the fact that children's awareness of the aims and reasons for psychological help is far greater than it used to be, still the contact with a psychologist is a greatly embarrassing matter. It mostly concerns students from older classes e.g., when they come to a psychologist to deal with some unimportant things they always take a friend with them to have a witness who can confirm that no advice or help was involved. Many children wait a few minutes after a bell till their peers go home so that nobody could see them entering a psychologist's room. Later they ask for a possibility of going out of the room before the bell because of the same reason.

Vast area of a psychologist's work are contacts with parents. Beliefs about mutual divergence between parents' and teachers' expectations are widely known (Sokołowska-Dzioba 2002). It happens that a teacher sends a parent to a school psychologist so that he/she solves a problem instead of this teacher. Sometimes a parent turns to a psychologist hoping that he/she will take over some problem and somehow influence a teacher. In a conflict situation a parent expects that a psychologist will take sides with him/her whereas a teacher expects a friendly support from us, which is one of many traps in this profession (Sałasiński & Badziukiewicz 2003).

A psychologist or pedagogue might help to prepare for a talk, might point out some methods of acting but the activeness stays at parents' side. That is why one has to remember to cooperate and not to do everything for other people.

Determining the conditions of an effective help for students in solving their school, personal, social or home problems, one cannot pass over the barriers that a school pedagogue has to encounter. Above all those barriers are:
- Taking on unfavourable roles (which were described earlier)
- Expectations (of headmaster, parents, teachers, school personnel and administration)
- Charging a pedagogue with difficult tasks
- Little support of pedagogical supervision and guidance.

School is a place where students gain information useful to assessing their own intellectual abilities, acquiring predispositions towards their future profession and deciding about their later education. In the beginning of this search there is a contact with a school pedagogue who at the same time is a tutor, carer, educator, diagnostician, and therapist. He/she must also remember not to cross the borders of his/her competence and to respect teachers', parents' or other specialists' competence but above all he/she has to be driven by students' sake. Help given at an appropriate time might satisfy a current need and not seldom might prevent deepening a problem. School is not only a place of spreading knowledge but also of caring for all students' needs.

References

Czajkowska, A. (1999): Nauczyciel – doradca, przyjaciel, terapeuta, In: W. Pilecka, G. Rudkowska & L. Wrona (eds.), Podstawy psychologii. Podręcznik dla studentów kierunków nauczycielskich, Kraków.
Firlit-Fesnak, G. & Szatur-Jaworska, B. (1995): Leksykon pojęć socjalnych, Warszawa.
King, G. (2003): Umiejętności terapeutyczne nauczyciela, GWP, Gdańsk.
Kodeks etyczno-zawodowy psychologa (2005): Polskie Towarzystwo Psychologiczne, Warszawa.
Kozdrowicz, E. (1995): Poradnictwo w teorii i praktyce, In: T. Pilch & I. Lepalczyk (eds.), Pedagogika społeczna, Warszawa.
Kozłowski, J. (1996): Nauczyciela zawód, Warszawa.
Nocuń, A.W. & Szmagalski, J. (1998): Podstawowe umiejętności w pracy socjalnej i ich kształcenie, Katowice.
PASW Code of Ethics (Kodeks Etyczny Polskiego Towarzystwa Pracowników Socjalnych).
Radlińska, H. (1961), Pedagogika społeczna, Warszawa.
Rozporządzenie Ministra Edukacji i Sportu z dn. 07 stycznia 2003
Sajdak, A. (2005): Porozumiewanie się w szkole na rzecz tworzenia edukacyjnej wspólnoty, Wydawnictwo Uniwersytetu Jagiellońskiego, Kraków.

Sałasiński, M. & Badziukiewicz, B. (2003): Vademecum pedagoga szkolnego, WSiP, Warszawa.

Sokołowska-Dzioba, T. (2002): Kształtowanie umiejętności wychowawczych, Lublin.

Strelau, J. (2000): Psychologia, T.3, GWP, Gdańsk.

Trojan, E., Wychowanie w szkole 2006/8

Ustawa o pomocy społecznej, Dz.U. Nr. 13 (1993) poz. 60, art. 8 p. 5.

www.basw.co.uk 2007-03-02

www.casw-acts.ca/practice/schoolsocialworker.htm 2007-03-02

www.psychologia.net.pl/artykul.php 2007-02-14; Maciejewska J., Ciało obce, psycholog w szkole,

www.sswaa.org/members/resolutions/training.thtml 2007-01-18

www.wshe.pl/ 2007-02-02; Mielczarek A., Dokąd zmierza praca socjalna XXI wieku,

Giving the Client a Voice
Child and Parent Participation in Youth Work

Peter Hansbauer

In the olden days, if you went to a garage, you would be able to buy petrol and perhaps basic items needed to keep your car on the road. Today, as I read recently, more ready-made pizzas are sold at garages in Germany than in any other shop. They now sell everything you would once have bought from the well-equipped grocery round the corner, including freshly baked bread. Conversely, you can now buy everything you need for a sumptuous breakfast, including eggs, bacon and your daily newspaper, from the delicatessen counter in your local bakery. Today, specialist shops and items which fulfil one specific purpose seem almost old-fashioned.

So why have I opened with this observation? I am recounting it as it exemplifies the fact that our society is rapidly being transformed into a 'multi-option society,' and indeed not only with regard to our own personal experiences. We experience and observe that this multi-optionality is becoming reified – it is becoming institutionalised, mechanised, it incorporates ever increasing expanses of our day-to-day life. The ability to choose between different alternatives has multiplied exponentially in our society.

Decision Making and Negotiating in Family Life

The mode by which alternative options are converted into real life, into actions, events or even directions in life is called decision making. This may sound abstract, but it is through decisions that we determine whether we, depending on our appetite, use our money to buy organic vegetables or to buy a ready-made pizza; whether we attend this or that school, because we consider ourselves – or our parents consider us – intelligent enough to attend it; whether we embark on this or that career or even what type of family support we find acceptable.

Just thirty years ago, the situation was substantially different. Back then, much was decided for us – by (supposed) authorities, by our parents, by our origins, by external conditions over which we had no control. Putting this positively, this means that, on average, individuals today have many more opportunities to choose that which best suits their lifestyles and their interests. Available alternatives can be precisely tailored to an individual's own needs or the needs of the individual on whose behalf decisions are being made. This potentially reduces the risk that unsuitable alternatives or support services will be utilised – unsuitable because they bypass the interests of the person involved. From a historical point of view, this is an opportunity which no previous generation has enjoyed to such an extent.

At the same time, the business of making decisions and adapting to individual needs is not that simple – making sensible decisions requires the ability (at least to some extent) to understand the consequences of these decisions. The capacity of many people, especially children, to do so is limited, so that they constantly find themselves out of their depth when faced with such decisions. Decision making must therefore be learnt and practiced, in a similar way to that in which a child learns and practices reading in order to be able to read books in later life. This requires opportunities for practice. Without opportunities for practice, it is not possible to learn to make decisions. Where something has not been learnt, situations where one is out of one's depth will inevitably occur, as when someone who has never learnt to read needs to read an instruction manual.

Decision making is made more difficult because there are – especially in the social field – very few decisions which affect us alone. Most decisions in our lives impact on other people. The career that I choose to embark on is frequently affected by my parents. Whether I accept this or that job offer may be affected by what my wife is currently doing or whether child-care facilities are available. Thus in our society decision making is often preceded by negotiation. Negotiation occurs in our professional lives, in our leisure time and in our everyday lives. We are forced to negotiate in situations in which we are unable to put our decisions into practice to the extent to which we would like, which would perhaps best serve our needs and interests. One can therefore say that, just as decision making must be learnt, so too must negotiation. Furthermore, in a society in which different lives are intimately intertwined, negotiation becomes a precondition for being able to take sensible decisions.

In normal families, this has long become the everyday reality. When describing changes to child-rearing practices within the family over the past thirty years, sociologists speak of an epochal transition from a "command household" to a "negotiation household" (Nave-Herz 2002, p. 68ff.). This means that in comparison to previous generations of children, today's children are given significantly more scope to act and have more power to make decisions over their own circumstances. Nowadays, children are taken far more seriously as negotiating partners and in general their wishes are respected to the greatest extent possible, even and in particular when it comes to negotiating rules within the family (cf. Sinus Sociovision GmbH 2004).

This epochal transformation in child-rearing styles follows – to an extent subversively – the transformed socio-functional requirements of an increasingly individualistic and at the same time more flexible society. This is because individualism means in principle nothing less than that decisions which in previous generations were pre-determined by social origins and tradition are now taken individually. This is precisely what the transition from a command to a negotiation household accommodates, because it systematically prepares and trains children and young people to negotiate, weigh things up, see things from the point of view of other people, make decisions and take responsibility for agreements which they have been involved in concluding. It should be noted that although systematically rehearsing negotiating methods and decision making strategies offers no guarantee of being able to successful cope with life, it is increasingly a pre-requisite for doing so. Both negotiating and decision making skills are needed in order to succeed in mastering the incredible diversity of options which life now offers.

But what does this have to do with the social services child protection and family support departments? In section 8 of Sozialgesetzbuch VIII (Social Security Code VIII, dealing with legislation relating to the provision of social services for children and young people), entitled "Participation of children and young people," the legislature has clearly codified this principle, as it has in section 36, which deals with the care planning process. The intention of the legislature is therefore that the term 'care planning' (*Hilfeplanung*) should be understood to directly refer to involvement of those affected, negotiation and joint decision making, involvement in negotiations over suitable forms of support, to negotiation with those affected on equal terms and to giving them the right to decide whether the support offered is appropriate and meets their needs, interests and expectations. Essentially, therefore, in drawing up Sozialgesetzbuch VIII, the legislature has merely reflected on and acknowledged what has already taken place elsewhere in society.

Why is Participation often so Difficult in Practice?

In principle, most professionals are well aware that in practice it is the service users who will decide whether or not to actually accept specific support. People are obdurate. While they can be exposed to a particular situation, it is not possible to force them to accept and positively evaluate that situation in such a way that the social support offered achieves its objectives. What is critical is not whether support is well-intentioned or even whether it is what is actually needed, rather it is that the person affected genuinely accepts that support and inwardly agrees to it.

In other words, social support is "client-controlled", in that service users decide whether they will actually buy into a particular arrangement (cf. Gross & Badura 1977; Gartner & Riessmann 1978; Schaarschuch 1999). Ultimately the 'fit' between the services or support offered and actual need will be the yardstick for the effectiveness and efficiency of support aimed at individuals (cf. Engel, Flösser & Gensink 1998). Failure to involve those affected significantly increases the risk that specific support will fail to achieve its objectives. In general it can be said that negotiated support tends to be better tailored to needs and therefore provide greater benefit. Allow me therefore, to now attempt to offer an answer to the question of why participation in the care planning process often presents difficulties in practice.

In the case of children and young people, a paradoxical requirement arises when we talk about participation (cf. Hansbauer & Schnurr 2002). We need to treat children and young people as if they are mature – i.e. they are able to take responsibility for determining their own interests – when in fact they are often not. It is not the case that minors are always able fully to comprehend the implications for them of certain decisions. Nor is it the case that we can always presume that what appears to be in their interests today will still be in their interests tomorrow. A reasonably stable set of interests on one side and a reasonably enlightened understanding of the consequences on the other are in fact pre-conditions for participation and co-determination. Even where children are, in this respect, capable of being involved in decision making, social workers are often required to make decisions on their behalf. Participation must therefore distinguish between articulated and actual needs. The two may coincide, but do not necessarily do so. What a child wants is not always what he or she needs. Participation – and this applies in particular for children and young people – frequently pre-supposes interpretation of needs, and in such a way that professionals must, in the best interests of the child, make such decisions as the child would be expected to take if he or she were a mature adult. The litmus test for the social worker in interpreting the needs of the child must thus be to ask, "Would the child, when he or she looks back at his or her life in a few years time, take the same decision as I am today taking on his or her behalf?"

Dealing with this paradox requires the social worker to be highly reflective. They must be able to distinguish whether the decision they propose to take is indeed in the best interests of the child – perhaps even against the interests expressed by that child – or whether they are perhaps merely convincing themselves that this is the case in order to conceal a lack of time resources, their own convenience, their own conception of a good life or organisational blind spots.

Participation of children and young people in the care planning process can therefore not simply be reduced to a procedural or legal requirement, however significant an instrumental knowledge of applicable methods and the procedural and legal frameworks may be. It is equally about respect for the life situations of others, about fairness, empathy, the ability to see things from another person's perspective and about transparency. In short, it is about a particular professional attitude. It is thus both a need for specific legal structures which permit and promote participation, for age-appropriate procedural methods such that children and young people are listened to and have the opportunity to formulate their own interests, and also a need for a certain socio-pedagogic professionalism – a professionalism which aims to avoid condescension, to take account of and engage with the interests and needs of children and young people and, with this in mind, attempts to take decisions in the best interests of the child (cf. Hansbauer & Kriener 2006).

The key to participation is that this socio-pedagogic professionalism or attitude must always come first. Structural, legal or procedural measures can never provide a substitute for such an attitude, since the care planning process in a specific situation is always based on a fundamental power divide, made up of at least three components.

There is firstly a *professionally determined power divide*, in that it is generally the professional who is in possession of legal and procedural knowledge and who provides his negotiating partner with information about this (or fails to do so as the case may be). It is also the professional who is aware of what services are available and makes proposals for suitable measures on the basis of this knowledge. This information is generally not available to his younger negotiating partner. Even where it is possible to resolve this informational difficulty, the advantage of experience still lies with the professional, who generally approaches the care planning process with a different perspective on the situation. For social workers in youth welfare services, the meeting with the client may be their 100th meeting. For the young person concerned it may be his or her first. Whilst the social worker is able to draw on experience from all these previous meetings, the client at whom the support is targeted has only his or her personal experience.

A second component of this power divide relates to the *person*. In contrast to most recipients of support, social work staff in youth welfare services are generally university graduates who have (or at least should have) learnt to express themselves with words, i.e. to frame their interests and expectations in words. They have also generally learnt to perform complex deliberations involving consideration of a number of differently weighted variables and they have ultimately also learnt how to present a sound argument so that it comes across as a sound argument. One cannot generally expect children and young people to possess these skills to the same degree.

Finally there is also a *situational power divide*. When young people present to youth welfare services, they are frequently preceded by a crisis situation or a conflict situation which has come to a head. For the recipient of support services, such crises are often of existential significance, for the social worker, they are part of his or her professional practice. On top of this, there is the fact that at the location where the procedure usually takes place, the client is in general a guest, the social worker, however, is essentially 'at home'. In a specific situation, this can often also make a significant difference.

While this situational power divide does not preclude negotiations on an equal footing, it does illustrate that such negotiations can only occur where the professionals involved are prepared to recognise the young client as an equal partner and to empower him or her to negotiate. The line between fair negotiation and manipulation when drawing up a care plan is thus a thin one, as the professional generally retains control over the procedure. Formal rules for participation therefore essentially change little, so that in fact it is the attitude of the professionals involved which represents the crucial factor, since, in view of this power divide, formal rules can always be undermined by social work staff.

Organisational Culture

Participation of children and young people in the care planning process is therefore not a simple requirement. It is not a simple requirement because it is not easy to formalise and to translate into departmental directives. Participation is always a question of the professional's attitude in dealing with children and young people. It is thus necessary, in calling for greater participation, to start by addressing the attitudes of the people who work in youth welfare services. The question needs to be asked, "How can the attitudes of the people within an organisation, how can the 'spirit' within an organisation or, more generally, the organisational culture, be fashioned such that it encourages participation of children and young people in decisions which primarily affect them?"

The paradigm of a specific "organisational culture" is based on the notion that the behaviour of a group is not shaped, influenced and often substantially guided solely by formal structures (generally written regulations concerning the way in which structures, tasks and procedures are organised), but equally by distinctive, implicit patterns of thinking and orientation. Organisational culture is therefore a generally held set of notions, which fulfils the function of guiding action where it is not possible to demand participation by means of service obligations and hierarchic specifications (cf. Lang, Winkler & Weik 2005, p. 209ff.). How is the effect of such an organisational culture to be pictured?

I will draw on a model by Schein (cf. Schreyögg 2003, p. 453, similar Merchel 2005, p. 167ff.), which distinguishes between three mutually interdependent and interacting levels of an existing organisational culture.

1. Fundamental or basic assumptions concerning environmental conditions, truths, conceptions of time, the nature of man and human action and the nature of interpersonal relationships.

Such fundamental or basic assumptions are at heart pre-scientific and acquired partly in parallel to or before practising one's profession (for example, because they have been conveyed as part of one's education). They are, however, also transmitted or modified as part of the process of professional socialisation. Most of these assumptions remain unspoken in everyday practice. We are often only dimly aware of them ourselves. What may at first sound rather abstract quickly becomes clear if we illustrate the effect of such fundamental, basic assumptions with an example.

Let us assume that 16-year old Joseph is accommodated in a residential facility and, in the process of formally reviewing his care plan, it is to be decided whether he should remain in his current residential home or whether he should move into a different type of residential facility or return to his mother. Let us further assume that 16-year old Joseph is accommodated in a residential home and that there are numerous reports and professional opinions on his history and behavioural difficulties, most of them tending to the negative. Finally, let us assume that this Joseph generally responds with obduracy when addressed directly and otherwise shows little appetite for integrating himself into group life, that, however, he sometimes immerses himself for hours on end in tasks of his own devising, the point of which is not at first sight apparent (for example, he recently spent an entire afternoon decorating his trousers with patches and other distinctive features). In conjunction with Joseph, a course of action for the future is now to be considered.

The social services child protection and family support department's decision will undoubtedly be influenced by the cost situation and by the extent to which there is pressure to take a particular decision. These agency-related environmental conditions have little to do with Joseph, but are clearly not without relevance for the overall assessment of the situation. A further question arises as to how the records and reports pertaining to Joseph should be used in the decision-making process. As with all academic or empirically acquired knowledge, the significance placed on such documents will vary depending on notions of how expert knowledge should be dealt with in principle, of whether one should trust and accept the "truth" of experts or should rely more on one's own experiences in dealing with Joseph, on one's own construction of "truth". Furthermore, the assessment will by influenced by considerations of the right time scale for interventions. When is the right time to act? When does a problem become urgent? What are the criteria for urgency? Basic notions of the nature of man, of whether man is conceived as being open to learning or as a being which is resistant to development and is defined by its past, are also likely to be not irrelevant in making this decision. Likewise notions of the sense of human action – from which it follows that the interpretation of the fact that Joseph dedicates himself for hours on end to tasks of his own devising, the point of which is not at first sight apparent, may vary widely. And not least, the fact that Joseph fails to integrate into group life and maintains a degree of self-reliance and obduracy can, depending on whether integration and submission are considered of fundamental value or whether the professionals involved are of the opinion that every person has a right to their individuality, be interpreted in widely differing ways.

These are all pointers to the effect of such fundamental, basic assumptions. They form the backdrop against which decisions and interventions will be made. It is a feature of such assumptions that they are, on the whole, not open and negotiated, but are invisible and generally also unconscious. Nonetheless, as unconscious and unspoken values, notions, images, preferences, etc., they play a crucial role in our everyday actions.

2. Norms and standards. In contrast to fundamental, basic assumptions, norms and standards are frequently visible and observable. They are reflected in the structures and procedures of the organisation and are manifest in the form of legal regulations, organisation charts, departmental directives, SOPs or protocols. However, not all norms and standards are reflected in such formal structures. There are a multitude of unwritten rules on how to deal with recurring situations.

These make it possible for individuals to distinguish between "correct" and "incorrect" courses of action and are often learnt in the course of day-to-day practice – by looking over the shoulder of more experienced colleagues or simply asking them how a particular situation should be dealt with.

3. Symbol system. In contrast to the above, this element of "organisational culture" is directly accessible to observation. The meaning of symbols is, however, not always immediately and directly apparent, and must often be interpreted with reference to the factors described above. Seating arrangements – whether everyone is seated around a round table or whether one person is entrenched behind a desk and the others are thus forced into the position of supplicants – are the expression of a particular organisational character. Whether the rooms look old and grubby or new and well-cared for, whether people wear suits and ties or are dressed casually, whether the tone with which people interact is relaxed or formal – all these things permit conclusions to be drawn about organisational culture. These symbols conceal values and relevance structures which allow seasoned observers, people with a certain amount of prior knowledge, to quickly draw conclusions about the culture of an organisation.

Although each of the three levels described has its own dynamic, if only because developments on each level generally occur at different times, these three dimensions cannot be considered and shaped in isolation, as there is mutual interaction between them. The organisational sociologist Karl E. Weick (1976) describes interactions of this nature, in which there is an internal, but not precisely definable, relationship as "loose couplings".

In shaping an organisation, it is, however, possible to utilise this internal relationship. Precisely because these three dimensions are mutually interactive, it can be assumed that changing norms and standards – the element of organisational culture which is most amenable to deliberate control – will also lead to changes on the other two levels. Just as fundamental, basic assumptions influence the norms and standards within an institution, so norms and standards influence the formation and sustained establishment of a particular symbol system and particular fundamental, basic assumptions. It is important to be aware of differences in the pace at which such changes occur, however. Whilst norms and standards and, to an extent, symbolic action can be changed relatively quickly, changing fundamental, basic assumptions is a long-term process, which may take many years.

Creating a Participation-Centred Organisational Culture

So far we have argued, firstly, that participation and negotiation increase the beneficial function of family support both with regard to socio-functional requirements and with regard to individual willingness to accept social support.

Secondly, that the requirement for participation cannot be reduced to formal, legal or procedural factors, but requires a reflective social worker with a specific attitude. In the absence of such an attitude there is a high risk that formal regulations will be undermined.

Thirdly, that the culture of an organisation influences the behaviour of individuals within that organisation.

Fourthly, that the components of an organisation's culture, i.e. the fundamental, basic assumptions, norms and standards and a specific symbol system, are mutually interactive.

Against this backdrop, we now need to pose the question of how these three levels of organisational culture can be shaped and influenced so that the result is a participation and co-determination-centred organisational culture. There is certainly no patent remedy or simple, quick, exhaustive solution. If success is achieved in directing impulses for change at all three levels of organisational culture towards a specific goal, this is likely to be highly beneficial for pushing organisational culture in the direction of greater participation and co-determination in the longer term. Creating such an organisational culture is first and foremost a management role.

The simplest of these factors to change is undoubtedly norms and standards – by means of an appropriate legal framework and appropriate departmental directives and SOPs handed down by the management of the social services agency in question. These may relate both to adherence to specific procedural standards or to good practice. This is important, not because it involves yielding to the illusion that it will produce a sudden cultural change, but because it moves the goalposts with regard to accountability. As an example, here in Germany, for the past 15 years we have had a relatively participation-centred legislative framework relating to children and young people. To date, it must unfortunately be said – and this is an opinion which is shared right up to the highest levels of government – that the 'spirit' of the law, the intention of the legislature to see social services child protection and family support established as a genuine service for children, young people and families has, in many agencies, not yet been realised. What this act has changed, however, is that people who contravene this legislation are frequently required to account for their actions. There is therefore an ongoing debate about the fact that applicable norms and standards are not being adhered to. The debate about norms and standards in itself means that they remain in the professional eye and are brought into sharper focus. In the long term – mighty oaks from tiny acorns grow – this fosters a greater awareness of norms and standards within an organisation.

Changing symbol systems within organisations is harder. Approaches to making such changes could initially consist of changing outward appearances, designing locations and situations so that they are more inviting and encourage participation, or providing appealing and comprehensible information. One participant at a conference exemplified this point as, "What has McDonalds got that we haven't?" The short answer, "Because children at McDonalds are wooed as customers, because the decor, look and style of communication are tailored to children and young people." Further measures might therefore include signalling readiness to engage with the needs of children and young people by means of the style of communication, making an effort to be polite, respectful and empathic, exuding trust, authenticity and openness. In other words, it is necessary to signal to children and young people through external appearances that you are interested in them as people. If this occurs, it is also likely to feed back into norms and basic assumptions.

Strategies for change aimed at changing fundamental, basic assumptions are comparably difficult to implement. Firstly, because this is usually a long term process. Secondly, because such basic assumptions frequently remain unconscious and the extent to which they can be discussed openly is therefore limited. And thirdly, because the extent to which they can be directly addressed and the extent to which the substance of change can be monitored is limited.

One can of course hope that simply changing the first two levels will lead to changes in basic assumptions over time. At the same time, one can support and promote such processes, by firstly continuously confounding existing pre-conceptions, and secondly, crudely put, by feeding new basic assumptions into the organisation in order to ensure the availability of alternative interpretive frameworks and patterns of behaviour.

Perturbation can be stimulated through supervision, practice guidance and research or forms of self-evaluation. It can also be stimulated through targeted staff selection, input from interns and practice placement students, by changing job descriptions or through job rotation. It is first and foremost the role of management to select and combine the instruments of perturbation so as to ensure that basic assumptions are continuously being shaken up.

The likelihood that alternative interpretive frameworks will be available to the organisation is increased if, for example, different levels of education and different professions are represented in the staff team, if appropriate literature is used, if different staff attend a variety of training courses relevant to their work and if organisations repeatedly attempt to depict what they are doing in publications. Writing helps order thought, clarify trains of argument and thus contributes to the refinement and differentiation of knowledge.

In contrast, factors which can hinder modification of basic assumptions include too small or too large groups of staff in close communication with each other, time constraints hindering communicative interaction, low motivation and a general low level of staff qualifications. Similarly, the presence of people with too much informal power, constantly imposing their points of view and opinions and suppressing other points of view, can also present an obstacle (cf. Klatetzki 1998).

Discussion of, and processes for reaching agreement regarding how requirements for participation should be dealt with in specific situations are crucial for both perturbation and for introducing alternative interpretive frameworks and patterns of behaviour. While, as discussed above, it is not possible to address fundamental, basic assumptions – which may be expressed through particular attitudes – directly, it is possible, through recurring discussion processes, to increase openness and willingness to examine one's own actions and to become more sensitive to the needs of children and young people.

References

Engel, M., Flösser, G. & Gensink, G. (1998): Quality-Enhancement in the Service Society: Perspectives for Social Work, In: G. Flösser & H.-U. Otto (eds.), Towards More Democracy in Social Services (pp. 357-370), Berlin/New York.

Gartner, A. & Riessman, F. (1978): Der aktive Konsument in der Dienstleistungs-gesellschaft, Frankfurt a.M.

Gross, P. & Badura, B. (1977): Sozialpolitik und soziale Dienste: Entwurf einer Theorie personenbezogener Dienstleistungen, In: C. von Ferber & F.X. Kaufmann (eds.), Soziologie und Sozialpolitik (Sonderheft 19 KZfSS) (pp. 361-385), Obladen.

Hansbauer, P. & Kriener, M. (2006): Erziehung braucht eine Kultur der Partizipation, In: Diakonieverbund Schweicheln e.V. (ed.), Erziehung braucht eine Kultur der Partizipation (pp. 9-34), Hiddenhausen.

Hansbauer, P. & Schnurr, S. (2002): Riskante Entscheidungen in der Sozialpädagogik. Ein Versuch zur Operationalisierung des pädagogischen Takts am Beispiel der „Straßenkinder" – Problematik, In: Zeitschrift für Erziehungswissenschaft, 5, 73-94.

Klatetzki, T. (1998): Qualitäten der Organisation, In: J. Merchel, (ed.), Qualität in der Jugendhilfe: Kriterien und Bewertungsmöglichkeiten (pp. 61-75), Münster.

Lang, R., Winkler, I. & Weik, E. (2005): Organisationskultur, Organisationaler Symbolismus und Organisationaler Diskurs, In: E. Weik, & R. Lang (eds.), Moderne Organisationstheorien 1 (pp. 207-258), Wiesbaden.

Merchel, J. (2005): Organisationsgestaltung in der Sozialen Arbeit: Grundlagen und Konzepte zur Reflexion, Gestaltung und Veränderung von Organisationen, Weinheim/München.

Nave-Herz, R. (2002): Familie heute: Wandel der Familienstrukturen und Folgen für die Erziehung, Darmstadt.

Schaarschuch, A. (1999): Theoretische Grundelemente sozialer Arbeit als Dienstleistung, In: Neue Praxis, 29, 543-560.

Schreyögg, G. (2003): Organisation. Grundlagen moderner Organisationsgestaltung, 4th ed., Wiesbaden.

Sinus Sociovision GmbH (2004): Erziehungsziele und -stile von Müttern mit kleinen Kindern: Pilotprojekt in den Sinus-Milieus Postmaterielle, Moderne Performer, Experimentalisten, Hedonisten, Heidelberg.

Weick, K.E. (1976): Educational Organizations as Loosely Coupled Systems, In: Adminstrative Science Quarterly, 21, 1-19.

The Biopsychosocial Model for Health, Disorder, Disease, and Disability

Consequences for Social Work Theory and Practice

Bernhard Brugger and Leander Pflüger

1. Preliminary Remarks

1.1 Preamble

In Germany approximately 30% of all social workers work in community and public health and it is foreseen that this number will increase in coming years. These social workers will be confronted with clients with mental health, developmental or behavioural problems, or those suffering from disability or acute or chronic disease.

In this work, social workers must not only co-operate with members of other professions; they must also compete with them. The social worker will come in contact with (e.g.) doctors, nurses, care workers, occupational therapists, speech therapists, physiotherapists and psychologists.

All of them have specific approaches to health, disorder, disease, and disability.

Generally we have three established models:

a) The *biomedical model* (also known as the *pathogenetic model*), in which health and disease are strictly separated and defined in terms of one another: "disease is the absence of health" and vice versa.

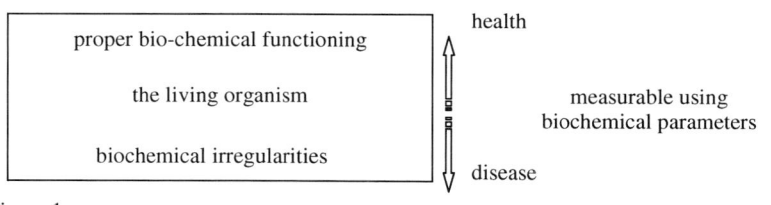

Figure 1

b) The *psychosomatic model*, in which health and disease arise as a result of the interplay between physiological and psychological factors, or indeed patho-physiological and psychopathological factors.

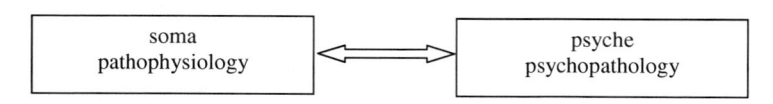

Figure 2

c) The *biopsychosocial model* that stresses the interplay between three types of factors – biological, psychological and social factors which are relevant regarding
   – causes (aetiology), conditions or triggers
   – symptoms, phenomenology or current conditions
   – prognosis, impact or consequences.

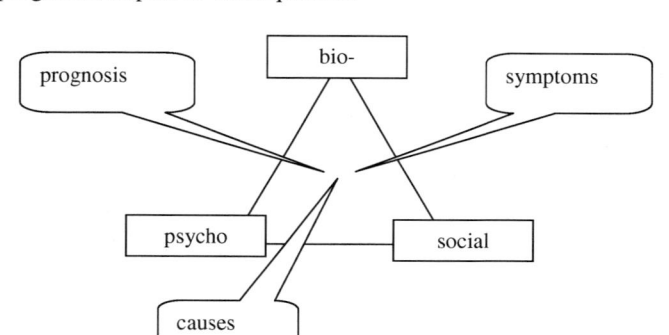

Figure 3

The "biopsychosocial model" is being increasingly advocated in scientific/academic literature. There are good reasons for this frequent citation.

However, not only laymen but also professionals continue to orient themselves around the *"biomedical model"*. Since this model describes disease, disorder and disability primarily as a result of biological (biochemical, physiological, physical, material) causes, biomedical measures are the primary treatment.
Psychological and social factors are relegated to the status of secondary and tertiary aspects. This clear hierarchy is then reflected in a corresponding hierarchy of the various professions.

Social workers employed in community health settings are calling for *"clinical social work"* to be recognised as a discipline in itself. As its reference point they cite the *"biopsychosocial model"*. In doing so, they are making a clear statement regarding health policy and the relationship between the various public health professions: they are *demanding the equal status of biological, psychological and social factors – and the equal status of the relevant professional groups.*

At the same time clinical social work practitioners note that the biopsychosocial model must form a part of the theoretical and practical basis of all social work. Some authors even go as far as to refer to a "forerunning role for clinical social work". In a discussion of a recently published book on "clinical social work" (Geissler-Piltz, Mühlum & Pauls 2005) Heiko Kleve assures the authors that they would be achieving something "not only necessary for clinical social work, but social work in general. They outline the particular perspective of the social work view and practice as distinct from that of other professions (...)" (Kleve 2005).

1.2 Objectives

This article will attempt to answer the following question: *What understanding of the biopsychosocial model do social workers need to acquire during their training* in order to be able to work together with (and successfully assert themselves against) other occupational groups? Even when social workers are not working in a therapeutic context, but rather "only" a counselling or care one, they will need a basic understanding of the relevant disorders, diseases and disabilities. What are the causes, what can have a positive or negative effect on recovery, what preventative measures can be taken?

Clinical social work practitioners note the effect of social factors upon psychological and biological factors. This justifies the necessity of not only clinical social work, but social work in general. Our key question in this article is thus: what knowledge of biological or medical processes must social workers have at their disposal, in order to participate fully, and make a contribution which is heard and acknowledged in an interdisciplinary setting? We claim that only social workers with a basic understanding of biology in a wider sense can fully represent "their own" component, namely the social one.

The idea here is of course not to make social workers into "semi-doctors", "semi-nurses" or similar, but rather to provide them with the training *needed to enable productive participation in interdisciplinary work*. Interdisciplinary work demands at least a working knowledge of the different ways of thinking and reacting to various problems.

A note about the authors: with our respective backgrounds of psychological psycho-therapy and special needs, we haven't strictly had a social work occupational socialisation. Nonetheless, we have been committed to social work for more than ten years now. We believe that participation in interdisciplinary work is one of the main characteristics of social work.

1.3 Outline

Firstly we will clarify the terms "biopsychosocial model" and "interdisciplinary thinking and practice". Although the term "biopsychosocial model" sounds unambiguous, it is well worth looking at the range of implications the term throws up.

Secondly, we will cite short case studies from two different areas: a) social work supporting a family where the mother is suffering from a major depressive episode; b) special needs support for a child with a severe learning disability.

Thirdly, building on these examples we will consider what canon of knowledge and basic skills social work students need to acquire in the course of their general basic training. The aim of this canon of knowledge is to qualify the social worker for interdisciplinary thinking and trans-disciplinary practice, in particular in community health settings.

We will not talk about the specific training programme of clinical social work (this separate training is only offered in a small number of German universities). Similarly, we are not concerned here with 'social therapy' (since January 2002 available on Germany's public health insurance schemes), despite its important role in consolidating the (self-)image of clinical social work in the future.

Fourthly, as far as initial investigation is concerned, we will look at the current training for social workers. In this context we are interested in looking beyond our own universities and national boarders. We would like to learn more about training in other countries. In our opinion – at least in Germany – there are at the present time the best opportunities for developing social work and gaining an equal status – equal to that of other professional groups.

2. The Terms: "Biopsychosocial Model" and "Interdisciplinary Thinking and Practice"

2.1 The Biopsychosocial Model

Broadly speaking, the biopsychosocial model makes the assumption that three factors, namely biological, psychological and social factors are responsible for causing, triggering or prolonging health, disease, disorders and disabilities.

These three somewhat schematic factors can be more precisely described:

- biological factors = physical, organic, somatic, genetic, sensory/neuro-physiological, biochemical, neuronal, hormonal/endocrine factors (basically ranging from the cellular level to the entire biological organism),
- psychological factors = innerpsychological processes; the conscious and the unconscious; wanting, feeling, thinking and action (volition, motivation, cognition including perception and attention, gross and fine motor skills), personality, individuality, construction of a subjective world,
- social factors = the interpersonal dimension, relationships, family relationships, social groups, cultural factors, economic and ecological environments, as well as the material environment.

The following illustration enables an initial overview:

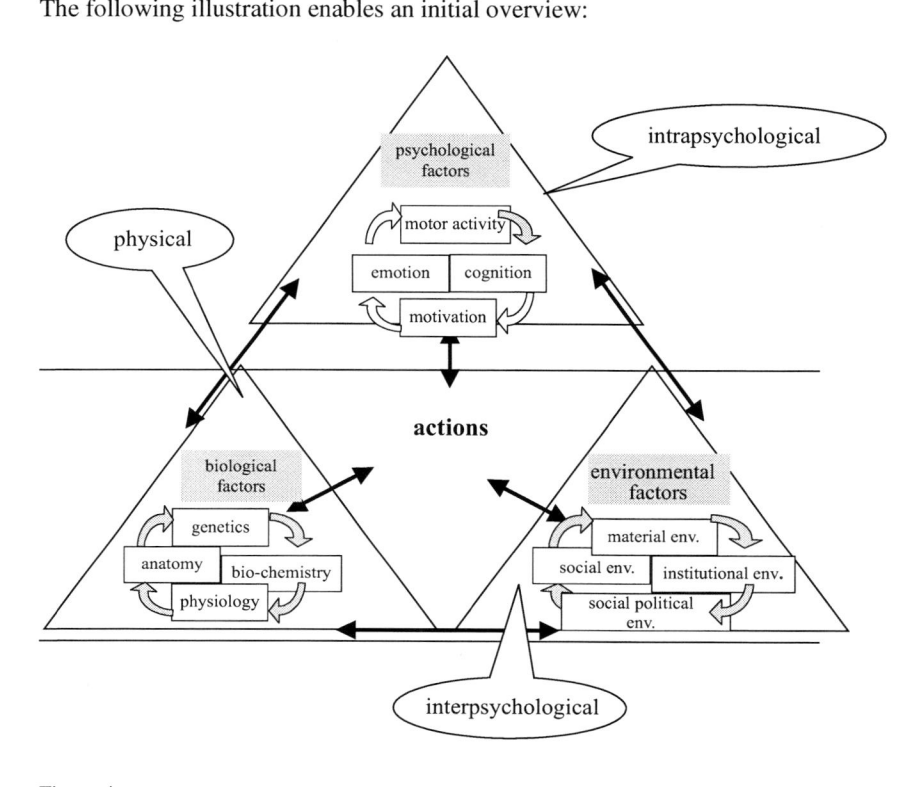

Figure 4

Please note: The third factor, social, is understood in the broad sense of all conditions surrounding the person.

Psychological and social factors are often combined in the expression "psycho-social" as a contrast to biological. Disagreement between the somatic and psychological schools regarding the "somatogenesis" or "psychogenesis" of disorders and diseases were common, and there was also disagreement concerning the importance of genetic and environmental factors. Today most academics recognise that all factors – in a complex interplay – impact on each other. Nonetheless, there do exist groups with vested interests, who stress one factor above the others: e.g. the pharmaceutical industry, some professional bodies – and indeed, many of us, as individuals: are organic causes for suffering not more agreeable than other reasons, such as an unhealthy lifestyle or chronic inner conflict...?

The domination of the biological/ biomedical model owes a lot to the rapid progress in natural science based medicine at the turn of the nineteenth/ twentieth century. From a social medicine perspective, the debate between Max Pettenkofer (the founder of medical hygiene) and Robert Koch (the founder of modern bacteriology) is telling.

In the current debate around psychological disorders (whether anxiety disorders, affective disorders or others) they are linked to the discovery of metabolic disorders in the brain, e. g., a serotonin deficiency which is in turn medicated.

It is however "overlooked" that good nutrition, sufficient physical exercise, or indeed good conversation and stable relationships have a similarly positive effect on our brain metabolic functions.

It is now widely acknowledged that social factors influence biological and psychological ones. Geissler-Piltz, Mühlum and Pauls (2005, p. 100) refer to this: "Social attachments are a necessary regulator of the physiology and the neurostructural development."

The bitter fact that "the poor die earlier" is empirically proven. As far as the psyche is concerned, self-confidence, a strong sense of self, the ability to form relationships and a host of other factors are closely linked with the interpersonal experiences we have, particularly those with our primary attachment figures. As far as "healing" measures are concerned, the "relationship factor" is a considerable factor in recent psychotherapy research. It is verified that good relationships lead ultimately to neurochemical changes in the brain. (Magnetic resonance imaging procedures of neurobiology and neuropsychotherapy have provided clear proof here.)

Back to the biopsychosocial model: It does not only draw attention to the necessary consideration of diverse factors. It is often presented as a systemic model: The individual factors comprise structured systems that influence each other mutually.

The following factor structure (with aspects of a depressive disorder taken as an example) may be useful:
Biological, psychological and social factors are not only relevant regarding causes, triggers or reasons, but also regarding symptoms, phenomenology or current conditions as well as prognosis etc. Furthermore there is a complex interplay between all aspects: E.g. deprivation of reinforcers may be a consequence of lack of willpower, but also a consequence of absence of appetite or "bad" environments. And deprivation of reinforcers may lead to distorted patterns of thinking as well as to metabolic disorders.

		causes, triggers, reasons	symptoms, phenomenology, current conditions	prognosis, impact, consequences
bio-		metabolic disorder	absence of appetite	disease susceptibility
	psycho-	distorted patterns of thinking	lack of willpower	deprivation of reinforcers
	-social	"bad" environments	retreat from other people	lack of soft skills

Figure 5

But: What recognition do biological factors gain in the psychological-social professions? Are social workers and psychologists aware that they are getting an incomplete picture by only considering social or psychological factors? We stated earlier that for all fields of social work, all three factors need to be taken into account, since no one factor alone can be seen as a solitary "cause".

Examples of such complex problems could be:
- the primary school pupil who doesn't get enough fluid intake, complains of stomach ache, and has a poor attention span, even for simple tasks;
- the overstrained child who, upon closer inspection, displays unusual motor activity with associated "simultaneous movements";
- the young person who withdraws from his circle of friends and suffers from hearing problems and ringing in the ears following a sudden hearing loss;
- the markedly overweight young person, who is reluctant to move about and who mainly feeds on fast food (by the way: the poorer the people the worse their nutrition);

– domestic violence related to a child's "clumsiness and laziness", where it finally comes to light that the primary cause is the child's undiagnosed muscle dystrophy.

These examples clearly show that only interdisciplinary thinking and practice can lead to professional social work. For this reason, the following basic elements of interdisciplinary thinking and trans-disciplinary practice shall be discussed.

2.1 Interdisciplinary Thinking and Practice

Two mutually contradictory trends can be seen in current developments in the scientific and professional communities. On the one hand, we have an increasing differentiation through division of labour and specialisation. On the other hand, we are seeing an increasing amount of interdisciplinary and trans-disciplinary co-operation.

The following illustration shows this:

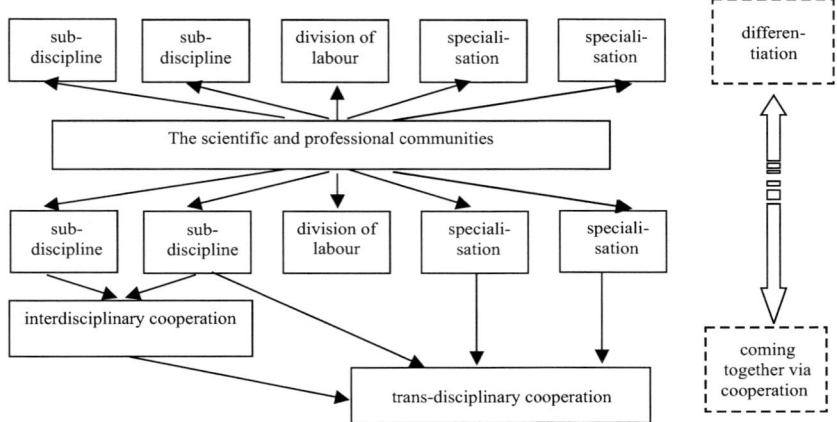

Figure 6

Co-operation is when at least two persons, groups or institutions work together in a way that is:
– planned
– goal oriented and
– rational, emotional, empathetic.

The term can also be described in terms of its negations: cooperation means no competition, no envy, no resentment, and no aggression.

Requirements for co-operation include the factors: setting, time, a shared assignment of tasks, shared values and norms on all levels of common practice (social-ethical, ecological-political).

Applied to the bio-psycho-social model this development results in the following:

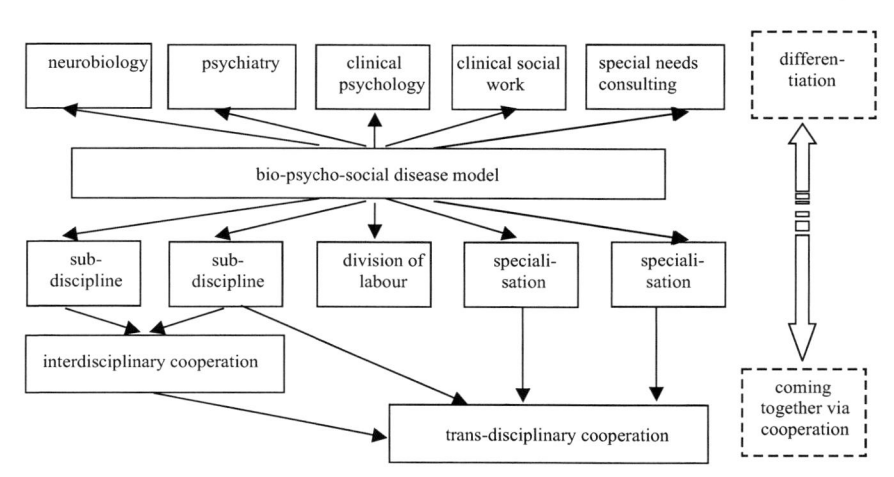

Figure 7

Should this model be applied to practice, it quickly becomes apparent that dealing with the two trends leads to two consequences:

Widening declarative knowledge on a form and content level and widening abilities on the communicative and social-interactional, organisational level (on the basis of so-called key qualifications)

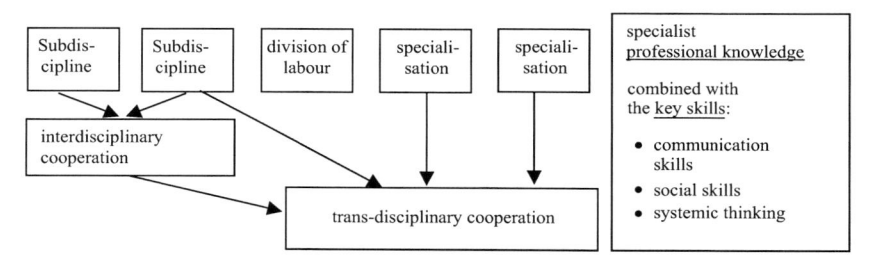

Figure 8

3. Case Studies

3.1 Case Study 1: Family with a Mother Suffering from a Major Depression (Social Work Assistance for the Family)

Imagine a social worker who, in the context of social work assistance for the family, is working with a single mother with two children of primary school age. She sees them approximately five hours per week. The initial contact was through a child support referral from the school.

The woman has been suffering from severe depressive disorder for a number of months. What should the social worker be prepared for? What must she know about the illness (i.e. the depressive disorder), in order to work with the mother and children? Not to be misunderstood: She will work as a social worker, not offer psychological or medical help. But she has to be aware of them and maybe initiate appointments with psychologists or psychiatrists.

We will put it a little bit provokingly:
- Is it sufficient to demonstrate understanding for the woman, who is constantly dropped by men, and who had a difficult childhood with a very authoritative father?
- Is it sufficient to organise shopping, to link in to help from the neighbourhood, to help the children with their schoolwork?
- Or must she have some knowledge of "depression", and mental health problems in general – at the very least, in order to answer the following questions from the mother, children or others:
  - How can it be explained that the mother is unable to respond to well-intentioned attempts to make conversation, suggestions to do activities, or pleasant gestures?
  - Why is she so inactive?
  - Is she lazy? – Is she really unable to be active, or is it a question of simply not wanting to?
  - What can have a negative impact on her depression?
  - How do people with depression impact on their family and how is it for the family members to have this contact?
  - Are family members responsible? What can they do wrong?
  - How do children react?

(Typical responses such as overcompensation, feelings of guilt, social withdrawal, parentification, i.e., when a child adopts an adult role before being emotionally or developmentally ready to do so ...)

Depression, particularly when chronic, cannot be fully understood without taking into account physical (neurochemical) processes. This is true of disorders even when these physical processes are not a primary cause. As an example of this, consider a heart attack. A heart attack can be caused by psychological-social factors (such as chronic stress, self-inflicted or from others). Nonetheless it first requires a somatic therapy. Then the focus can return to the psychological-social factors, with the objective of coping with the illness, and preventing relapse. In principle, the treatment of a depressive disorder works in the same way.

3.2 Case Study 2

Disabled child, "Nele", 2;4 years old – *film with spoken commentary*:

regarding social factors:
– she has no active verbal language
– she understands simple, everyday instructions
– when playing she has little relationship to her social partners

regarding psychological factors:
– her thinking is egocentric
– she shows little response to the behaviour of the social partner
– she signalizes wishes and anxiety
– she has astonishing good perception concerning her own body
– she presents many motor-stereotypes

regarding biological factors:
– her motor-skills are characterised by symmetric patterns
– there is no spontaneous rotation (there are exclusions)
– good functions in the parietal area
– imperfect functions in the frontal area (executive functions)
– imperfect functions in Wernicke and Broca area
– imperfect cooperation between cerebellum basal ganglia and cortex, limbic system and (frontal) cortex
– in the film she shows the patterns of the BNS-seizure; syn. *Propulsive Petit-mal*, West-Syndrome.

4. Canon of Basic Knowledge and Skills

4.1 With Reference to the Biopsychosocial Model

For an affective disorder, an initial collection of necessary basic knowledge derived from the biopsychosocial model would cover the following aspects:

–   A clear picture of possible relevant biological, psychological and social (environmental) factors, which can cause or impact upon affective disorders, or mental health problems in general;
    examples would be *(biological:)* neurotransmitter disorders of the brain; genetic disposition; environmental toxins; unbalanced nutrition; lack of exercise; side effects from medication // *(psychological:)* distorted patterns of thinking; lack of willpower // *(social:)* stress at the workplace or in the home environment; long-term unresolved conflict;
–   similarly, knowledge not only of the psychological and social problems associated with depression, but also of the somatic symptoms and physical consequences/complications;
–   even a depression of predominantly psychosocial origin will be accompanied by sleeping disorders, loss of appetite, loss of libido, weakening of the immune system; weight gain due to antidepressants
–   a knowledge of risk factors and protective factors, as in the vulnerability-stress model of disorder;
–   an idea why light activities such as going for short walks or talking with others are important.

For the case of the disabled child, an initial collection of necessary basic knowledge derived from the biopsychosocial model would cover the following aspects:

–   A clear understanding of relevant biological factors relating to sensory impairments;
–   neuropsychological and neuro-educational basic knowledge;
–   relevant knowledge of the biochemical processes which determine behaviour.

4.2 Basic Knowledge for Interdisciplinary Thinking and Practice

The following points are required:

a) Basic knowledge of the work of other occupational groups:
    How are other professionals trained? What are the important terms, paradigms, models of other disciplines? (E.g. knowledge of the specific subdisciplines of the medical sciences: what is psychiatry, what is neuro-psychiatry, what is neurology, what is psychosomatic medicine etc.)

b) Knowledge of the organisation of medical and psychological-social support; and: how are other occupational groups organised?
    (E.g. how does being freelance affect practitioners? Why do most psychiatrists have so little time for ambulant patients with psychological disorders?)

c) The ability to reflect on anthropological and ontological (metaphysical) questions (E.g. the mind-body problem which underlies the biopsycho-social model)

d) Knowledge of how one can gain access to (trustworthy) information in other disciplines (whether via the internet or in printed media. What must one know, to be able to critically analyse such media?)

e) The ability to think in multi-factoral and networked patterns of relations as opposed to simple linear ones

Regarding (e), multi-factoral and networked thinking: this means abandoning the idea that disability, disease or health can be explained in terms of a linear, mono-causal, cause-effect model. The correct view is a multi-factoral net of relations.

The analysis of this field of conditions, the clarification of the causal factors, the definition of a problem and the formulation of solution proposals cannot be done be one person alone – especially when help in the form of social work is needed. An interdisciplinary team is needed to fulfil these tasks.

– It should fill gaps in expertise.
– It should find tailor made solutions.
– It should find good solutions quickly.

This brings us to a closing discussion of the "ability to work in an interdisciplinary team".

Communication, co-ordination and an integration of knowledge constitute the three most important basic skills for a successful contribution to the work of an interdisciplinary team.

Communication: Specific communication rules govern interdisciplinary work. In an analogy to the concept of intercultural communication, we can speak here of interprofessional communication. This communication not only reflects norms and values, but also the expertise of those involved.

A central task is thus the establishing of a common set of terms (performance), closely coupled with the process of integration of knowledge (competence).

Co-ordination: This term brings together all tasks and processes organising interdisciplinary work. This includes, for example, clarification of who deals with which tasks when.

Integration of knowledge: This refers to the acquisition and establishment of a basic understanding of the discipline in question. We could formulate this differently: Integration of knowledge facilitates an understanding of the basic paradigms of the discipline in question.

These processes are largely a result of specific experience of the communication and co-ordination structures of interdisciplinary work. Integration of knowledge is, right from the beginning, a conscious process only for experienced practitioners. Inexperienced ones address this point first when conflict arises.

Integration of knowledge enables a change of perspective. The partner's objectives, ways of thinking and discussing can be learnt and internalised.

Dynamics around the triad of basic skills:

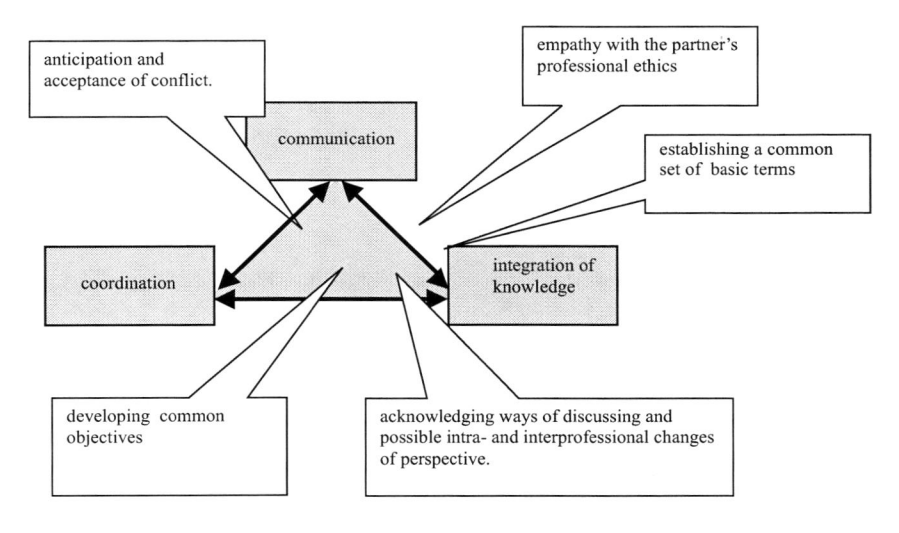

Figure 9

5. Conclusions

Preliminary research on the extent to which current social work training programmes take the biopsychosocial model into account and on how they qualify students for inter- and trans-disciplinary practice, generated deflating results. Even in post qualifying training courses on clinical social work, these topics are inadequately addressed.

Our findings are reflected in current German literature on clinical social work, community and public health social work, or social work in the field of psychiatry (e.g. Bosshard et al. [2]2001; Dörr 2005 & Geissler-Piltz et al. 2005). They often stress the importance of the biopsychosocial model or the importance of net-working.

Bosshard et al. (2001, p. 68) state: "The development of informal and formal cooperative connections (...) belongs to the tools. Furthermore, social workers should not underestimate their potential to act on changes of institutional structures and should be confident when trying to establish cooperative connections within interdisciplinary teams."

There is, however, a paucity of German language literature on the implications of the biopsychosocial model and about the question as to how social workers may be qualified for inter- and trans-disciplinary work.

In our opinion *the present time offers the best opportunities for developing the social work profession and securing it an equal status to that of other professional groups.*

For four reasons:
1. At the present time *social work degree courses are being re-structured.* The degrees given by universities and universities of applied sciences, especially Master's degrees, are becoming more and more aligned. Although the final form of new medical courses is still unclear, there is a real chance that a Master of Social Work will have the same standing as a Master of Psychology, provided that the Master of Social Work has clear goals. (Both degrees will have the same regular duration of study.)
2. *The social work profession could benefit from the "forerunning role of clinical social work"* (see chapter 0.1). There are also some parallels to be drawn with developments within the medical sciences, where new approaches are being seen – illustrated by the groundbreaking literature of Bernard Lown and David Servan-Schreiber (Lown 2004; Servan-Schreiber 2005). These new approaches are a response to the fact that medical sciences are increasingly being asked to treat chronic diseases and psychological disorders. Servan-Schreiber is himself a psychiatrist, and it is worth noting that the biopsychosocial model was first outlined by a psychiatrist, George Engel (1977).
3. *Modern health systems are likely to collapse and force societies to develop new structures.* It has been proved that one euro spent on social therapy (by clinical social workers) leads to savings of three euros. Last but not least, preventative work (and preventative social work) will become much more important.
4. *More and more practitioners (and academics) of traditional medicine are drawing attention to the limitations of the traditional biomedical model.*

They are increasingly pointing to the need for philosophical reflection. In the "Bayerische Ärzteblatt", February 2007, Prof. Felix Tretter, clinical centre München-Ost, laments the "considerable philosophical deficits" of a medicine which *"increasingly characterises itself as a medicine of repair, and the person as a biomolecular machine"* (Tretter 2007). He concludes: *"It seems that the only way forward is a revitalising of philosophy as an area where action is reflected upon"* (ibid.).

In the end, we touch here upon fundamental philosophical questions, in particular, those of anthropological and metaphysical nature. What does it mean to be human? How much can a human be seen as a mental-bodily being? What about the question of material or immaterial (ideal) "values"?

6. Discussion

We would like to discuss the development of social work in other countries:

- What role does the biopsychosocial model play? For social workers as well as for practitioners of other professions or laymen?

- How is social work integrated in the health system? – Is there a chance of establishing social work within the fields of community and public health?

- What kind of social work degrees (graduate, post-graduate or post-qualifying) are offered? – Are there any degrees similar to clinical social work? (e.g. the Mental Health Social Worker in the UK).

References

Bosshard, M., Ebert, U. & Lazarus, H. (^{2}2001): Sozialarbeit und Sozialpädagogik in der Psychiatrie. Bonn: Psychiatrie-Verlag.

Dörr, M. (2005): Soziale Arbeit in der Psychiatrie. München/Basel: Reinhardt.

Engel, G. (1977): The need for a new medical model: a challenge for biomedicine. In: Science, 196, 129-136.

Geissler-Pilitz, B., Mühlum, A. & Pauls, H. (2005): Klinische Sozialarbeit. München/ Basel: Reinhardt.

Kleve, H. (2005): Rezension zu B. Geißler-Piltz, A. Mühlum & H. Pauls: Klinische Sozialarbeit. Available at www.klinische-sozialarbeit.de/Rezension_Kleve_ UTB.pdf (15.02.07).

Lown, B. (^{2}2004): Die verlorene Kunst des Heilens. Anstiftung zum Umdenken. Stuttgart: Schattauer.

Servan-Schreiber, D. (^{11}2005): Die neue Medizin der Emotionen. München: Kunstmann.

Tretter, F. (2007): Materialistische Menschenbilder in der Medizin und der Bedarf an Philosophie. In: Bayerisches Ärzteblatt, 62 (2), 99.

Authors

Brugger, Bernhard, Prof. Dr., Psychotherapist, Lecturer at the University of Applied Sciences Münster, Germany
Main Focus: Clinical Psychology, Clinical Social Work, International Social Work

Duffy, Joe, Lecturer in Social Work at Queen's University Belfast, Northern Ireland
Main Focus: User Involvement in Social Work, Human Rights, Decision making and Citizenship Perspectives

Hansbauer, Peter, Prof. Dr., Social Worker, Sociologist, Lecturer at the University of Applied Sciences, Münster, Germany
Main Focus: Deviant Behavior, Family Sociology, Child and Youth Care

Jansen, Irmgard, Prof. Dr., Social Worker, Lecturer at the University of Applied Sciences, Münster, Germany (Head of the International Board)
Main Focus: Youth Delinquency

Kijowska, Iwona, Dr., Psychotherapist, Lecturer at the University of Humanities and Economy of Elblag, Poland
Main Focus: Educational Diagnostics and Therapy, Educational Councelling

Koht, Harad, Dr., Associated Prof., Lecturer at the Faculty of Social Sciences, Oslo University College, Norway
Main Focus: User Participation

Pantucek, Peter, Prof. Dr., Social Worker, Lecturer at the University of Applied Sciences St. Pölten, Austria
Main Focus: Theory and Methods of Social Work, Social Diagnostics

Pflüger, Leander, Prof. Dr., Special Education Teacher, Lecturer at the University of Applied Sciences, Münster, Germany
Main Focus: General Therapeutic Pedagogy, Clinical Neuropedagogy

Sorokosz, Irena, Dr., Psychologist, Lecturer at the University of Humanities and Economy of Elblag, Poland
Main Focus: Clinical Psychology, Councelling Psychology

Vogel, Christian, Prof. Dr., Social Worker, Lecturer at the University of Applied Sciences, Bern, Schweiz
Main Focus: Social Work in Schools

Zander, Margherita, Prof. Dr., Political Scientist, Lecturer at the University of Applied Sciences, Münster, Germany
Main Focus: Child Poverty, Gender, Resilienz

Waxmann

Forschung, Studium und Praxis

Schriften des Fachbereichs Sozialwesen der
Fachhochschule Münster

■ **Band 1**
Norbert Erlemeier

Alternspsychologie

Grundlagen für Sozial- und
Pflegeberufe

2002, 288 Seiten, br.
2. erw. Auflage, 19,50 €
ISBN 978-3-8309-1185-2

Diese Einführung in die Alternspsychologie vermittelt nicht nur Erkennt-
nisse heutiger Alternspsychologie, die
für die Soziale Arbeit mit alten Menschen fundierend sind, sondern sie
greift in die Diskussion über angemes-
sene Methoden der Altenarbeit und
Altenpflege ein.

■ **Band 2**
Günter Witzsch

Von Rio nach Kyoto

Die großen Umweltkonferenzen
der Vereinten Nationen in den
90er Jahren

1999, 151 Seiten, br., 15,30 €
ISBN 978-3-89325-766-9

Die Frage der Überlebensfähigkeit der
Menschen angesichts dramatischer
Umweltkrisen war Gegenstand der
drei wichtigsten umweltpolitischen
Konferenzen der Vereinten Nationen –
in Rio de Janeiro 1992, Kairo 1994
und Kyoto 1997. Der Autor hat an den
Konferenzen teilgenommen und kom-
mentiert hier ihre Ergebnisse.

■ **Band 4**
Luise Hartwig,
Joachim Merchel (Hrsg.)

Parteilichkeit in der Sozialen Arbeit

2000, 232 Seiten, br., 19,50 €
ISBN 978-3-89325-822-2

Dieser Band möchte die Diskussion
zum Parteilichkeitsbegriff aus unter-
schiedlichen Perspektiven anstoßen.
Zu diesem Zweck nehmen die Autorinnen und Autoren begriffliche Diffe-
renzierungen vor und fragen nach der
Tragfähigkeit des Parteilichkeitsbe-
griffs im Rahmen einer professionell
gestalteten Sozialen Arbeit. Damit
werden Impulse gegeben für die weite-
re – auch kontroverse – Verständigung
über den konzeptionellen und metho-
dischen Gehalt des Parteilichkeitsbe-
griffs in den verschiedenen Feldern der
Sozialen Arbeit.

■ **Band 5**
Horst Blatt, Karl-Heinz Grohall,
Friedhelm Höfener (Hrsg.)

Weiterbildung für Sozialberufe an Hochschulen

Perspektiven und Beispiele

2002, 248 Seiten, br., 19,00 €
ISBN 978-3-8309-1172-2

Diese Beiträge sind unmittelbar aus
dem Umfeld des Bereichs Weiterbildung am Fachbereich Sozialwesen der
Fachhochschule Münster entstanden.
Die Autorinnen und Autoren waren
auf unterschiedliche Weise an seiner
Entwicklung beteiligt und bringen in
ihren Beiträgen die dabei gewonnenen
Erfahrungen sowohl der konzeptionellen Arbeit als auch der praktischen
Durchführung ein.

MÜNSTER · NEW YORK · MÜNCHEN · BERLIN

Forschung, Studium und Praxis

Schriften des Fachbereichs Sozialwesen der Fachhochschule Münster

Waxmann

■ Band 6

Martin Doehlemann

Die Kreativität der Kinder

Anregungen für Erwachsene.
Mit einem Beitrag von
Norbert Rath

2001, 220 Seiten, br., 15,30 €
ISBN 978-3-8309-1032-9

Kinder sind schöpferisch – eher unbeabsichtigt und spielerisch planlos. Sie haben nicht selten wundersame poetische oder philosophische Einfälle, Geistesblitze, Gemütsregungen und Handlungsbedürfnisse. In diesem Band sind vielfältige *merk*würdige Lebensäußerungen von Kindern zusammengetragen, die zum Mitdenken und Miterleben einladen. Ein Buch für alle, die im Beruf, in der Freizeit und Familie einen für beide Seiten „lohnenden" Umgang mit Kindern suchen.

■ Band 7

Gregor Sauerwald, Brigitte Bauer, Sven Kluge (Hrsg.)

Kampf um Anerkennung

Zur Grundlegung von Sozialer Arbeit als Anerkennnungsarbeit

2002, 146 Seiten, br., 16,90 €
ISBN 978-3-8309-1156-2

Der Fachbereich Sozialwesen an der Fachhochschule Münster stellt in einem interdisziplinären Kolloquium das Anerkennungstheorem in seiner Anschlussfähigkeit an die Soziale Arbeit zur Diskussion. Das Ergebnis liegt hier vor: Soziale Arbeit als Anerkennungsarbeit. Damit wird das Konzept der internationalen Berufsverbände von Sozialer Arbeit als Menschenrechtsarbeit auf den Punkt gebracht.

■ Band 8

Martin Doehlemann (Hrsg.)

LebensWandel

Streifzüge durch spätmoderne Beziehungslandschaften

2003, 280 Seiten, br., zahlr. Abb., 16,90 €
ISBN 978-3-8309-1207-1

Nicht um „große" Abhandlungen zu verfassen, fanden sich zehn Sozial- und Geisteswissenschaftler/innen zusammen. In „kleiner" Form wollen sie sich dem Thema nähern, in Skizzen, Miniaturen, Streiflichtern – eher locker aufgesetzt, leicht lesbar und dennoch nicht ungenau oder inhaltsarm. Sie wollen aus vielfarbigen Splittern ein Mosaik zusammensetzen, ein buntes, nicht unbedingt widerspruchsfreies Bild der Vielfalt im Wandel geben.

■ Band 9

Stefanie Ernst (Hrsg.)

Auf der Klaviatur der sozialen Wirklichkeit

Studien – Erfahrungen – Kontroversen

2004, 248 Seiten, br., 29,90 €
ISBN 978-3-8309-1290-3

Von der Entwicklung der Sozialen Arbeit über den Bestand und Wandel von Organisationen bis zu Musik und Alter, von Armut über Drogenhilfepolitik bis zu Wohnungslosigkeit sowie vom Sozialwesen und Gesetzen bis zur fürsorglichen Kritik utopischer Rhetorik – erfährt der Leser einiges über das breite Spektrum sozialberuflichen Interesses.

MÜNSTER · NEW YORK · MÜNCHEN · BERLIN

Waxmann

Forschung, Studium und Praxis

Schriften des Fachbereichs Sozialwesen der
Fachhochschule Münster

■ Band 10

Wigbert Flock, Hans-Joachim
Jungblut, Agustín Lapetina,
Bernarda Monestier,
Gregor Sauerwald (Hrsg.)

Kinder- und Jugendhilfe in Deutschland und Uruguay auf der Suche nach neuen Formen methodischen Handelns

2004, 366 Seiten, br.
spanisch und deutsch, 25,50 €
ISBN 978-3-8309-1391-7

Dieser Sammelband – Ergebnis eines
gemeinsamen Forschungsprojektes der
Fachhochschule Münster und der Uni-
versidad Católica del Uruguay – ana-
lysiert die sozialen Folgen der Globali-
sierung für Kinder und Jugendliche.

■ Band 11

Kuhrau-Neumärker, Dorothea

„War das o.k.?"

Moralische Konflikte im Alltag
Sozialer Arbeit

2005, 230 Seiten, br., 19,90 €
ISBN 978-3-8309-1330-6

„War das o.k.?" – „Handelte ich
falsch?" Das sind ethische Fragen, die
sich auch Angehörige helfender Beru-
fe immer wieder stellen. Den Ärzten
sollte darauf einmal der Hippokra-
tische Eid antworten. Er wird in diesem Buch durch kurze Texte und Ar-
gumente von Platon bis Habermas so
interpretiert, dass er auch Sozialarbei-
terinnen in den Konflikten ihrer Be-
rufspraxis als Orientierung dienen
kann.

■ Band 12

Irmgard Jansen,
Wolfgang Rüting,
Hans-Jürgen Schimke (Hrsg.)

„Anwalt des Kindes"

2005, 252 Seiten, br., 19,90 €
ISBN 978-3-8309-1548-5

1998 hat der Gesetzgeber die Mög-
lichkeit der eigenständigen Vertretung
von Minderjährigen in familiengerichtlichen Verfahren durch den § 50 FGG
gesetzlich geregelt. In diesem Gesetz
spiegelt sich die Einsicht wider, dass
Kinder und Jugendliche als Betroffene
in einer familiengerichtlichen Ausein-
andersetzung speziellen fachlichen
Beistand benötigen. Zur Ausgestaltung
der Verfahrenspflege nach § 50 FGG
gibt es bis heute jedoch weder einheit-
liche Standards zur Qualifizierung
noch klare Vorstellungen zur Rolle
und zum Tätigkeitsprofil der Verfah-
renspfleger/-innen.
Dieser Band nimmt eine deutliche
Positionsbestimmung der Verfahrenspflege nach § 50 FGG vor. In diesem
Sinne argumentieren die Autorinnen
und Autoren – vor dem Hintergrund
unterschiedlicher Disziplinen – für
eine parteiliche Rolle der Verfahrenspflege im familiengerichtlichen Verfahren als „Anwalt des Kindes". Mit
dieser deutlichen Verortung leistet der
Band einen notwendigen Beitrag zur
aktuellen Fachdiskussion, ermöglicht
eine Praxisorientierung für tätige Ver-
fahrenspfleger/-innen und gibt Impulse
für Fort- und Weiterbildung.

MÜNSTER · NEW YORK · MÜNCHEN · BERLIN